RUNNING OVER ROCKS

Ian Adams is a poet, writer, artist and retreat leader. He is author of *Cave Refectory Road* (Canterbury Press, 2010) and creator of the daily Morning Bell on social media. Ian is a director of StillPoint, a project seeking to nurture contemplative spiritual practice, and a partner in the Beloved Life project exploring how spiritual practice may change the world. He is an Anglican priest, an Associate Missioner for Fresh Expressions, and Missional Community Developer with CMS. He lives in South Devon.

RUNNING OVER ROCKS

Spiritual practices to transform tough times

Ian Adams

CANTERBURY
PRESS
Norwich

© Ian Adams 2013

First published in 2013 by the Canterbury Press Norwich
Editorial office
3rd Floor, Invicta House,
108–114 Golden Lane,
London EC1Y 0TG.

Canterbury Press is an imprint of Hymns Ancient & Modern Ltd

All rights reserved. No part of this publication may be reproduced,
stored in a retrieval system, or transmitted,
in any form or by any means, electronic, mechanical,
photocopying or otherwise, without the prior permission of
the publisher, Canterbury Press.

The Author has asserted his right under the Copyright, Designs and
Patents Act, 1988, to be identified as the Author of this Work.

British Library Cataloguing in Publication data

A catalogue record for this book is available
from the British Library

978 1 84825 168 7

Typeset by Regent Typesetting, London
Printed and bound in Great Britain by
CPI Group (UK) Ltd, Croydon

Contents

Poems

POEMS

For James, Esther and Rachel

Unexpected sunshine one January morning at North Sands – the bay where the poem 'Running over rocks' began to form. The woman's gesture and the moment seemed full of possibility. What might be coming into being?

Introduction

RUNNING OVER ROCKS

Running over rocks I remember
as a child, shoreline boulders taller
than me, and my leaving and landing
one-easy-blur-of-movement.

The faster I went the freer I became
so natural, sensing each footfall place
without knowing how or why,
the earthbound rock full of life
pitching me into flight –
a surface-skimming bird
laughing at the brilliance of it all
the sunlight, the sea, this supple body
singing

But now running over rocks
is just a memory and all I see are cracks
and crevasses dark and deep,
detritus strewn in the choking tide.
No easy movement now. Only
slow   cautious   steps
imagining my falling
the thud of head on rock
a nauseous slide into unconscious
drowning in blood and water.

Running over rocks.
I want to move this way again
light and free
laughing at the brilliance of it all
the sunlight, the sea, this supple body
singing

Blessed are the pure in heart, for they will see God.

A teaching of Jesus: Matthew 6.8

The Great Task?

What might be the great task for our time? In our quest for survival as human beings through the demands of existence we can find ourselves forgetting to ask this question. Other urgent needs demand our attention. Most of the time we are just trying to get by! But this question may reveal the possibility not only of our survival, and that of the planet, but also of our flourishing. So what might be re-orientation required of us now, the movement to be entered into, the new song to be sung? What is the great task for you, for me, and for all human beings?

The most insightful response may be that the task is as it always has been. The song remains the same for each of us and for all of us: to live at peace with ourselves, with love for our neighbour and in love with the love that holds everything, which many call God. And so *to be goodness and to bring goodness* to our fellow human beings, to our fellow creatures, and to the planet. To live with imagination, adventure and generosity[1] *for* and *in* a world that frequently threatens to extinguish each of these truly human characteristics. This is the task of *becoming truly human*.

And the task begins in rediscovering who we are and where we belong. We need to come home to ourselves, and to recover our deep connection with all that exists. We need to rediscover the nature of our own mystery, and to rediscover the nature of the greater mystery of which we are part – existence itself. This rediscovery will encompass all of life, from whatever seems most 'normal' to whatever seems most 'sacred'. It will enable us to negotiate life however it comes to us, in all its wonder and joy, toughness and disturbance. And it will draw on everything that we have experienced in life up this to moment. Everything is learning!

---

1 A line of Gail Adams – www.theseechange.info.

The Art of Running Over Rocks

Bare rock, the sun on my back. I find a hand-hold, and pull myself up. Scattered in front of me along the beach, like debris from a game of some playful ancient giants, is a field of huge grey-black volcanic boulders. I take a big step onto the next boulder. Then another, and now a jump. Happy surprise, this is easier than I thought it would be. More steps, more boulders. I begin to move with more fluidity. Then comes a revelation. The faster I move the more natural is my movement. The less I think about the path, the clearer the path becomes. The less I calculate the route, the more easily my feet seem to find it. With the sea at my side, and the sun warming my back, laughter comes. I am on the edge of emerging from childhood into adolescence. Most days this young season of life has felt like an awkward process, but in this moment on this day I feel free. I'm running over rocks.

Forward to another summer's day many years later. Watching the sea surge over other boulders on another beach, on the south-west coast of England. In the clarity of the light shining through the sea-spray I suddenly realize that, decades on, the art of *running over rocks* isn't coming so naturally. There are some days when all I'm doing is looking down, all I'm seeing are the deep gaps be-tween the boulders, their dangerous edges and their impossible walls. The toughness of life can sap from us our ability to move through it with joy, grace and purpose. When disturbances come we can find ourselves closing up. We lose our momentum and our confidence. The imagination that opens up new possibilities fades. And we stop being generous, carefully guarding whatever we have unless this too is taken from us. This dehumanizing process hap-pens to individuals, to communities, to whole societies. If we are to re-engage with the great task of our time – to be goodness and to bring goodness to the world – this needs our urgent attention.

A Life of Spiritual Practice

Running Over Rocks is an invitation into a journey of discovery. Through poems, images and reflections it imagines how we might craft a series of spiritual practices, to enable us to live in the twenty-first century with joy, grace and purpose through both good times and tough seasons. To help us to look up and travel our path more easily, to keep our balance in life, even when everything threatens to overwhelm us. To hold us through the ups and downs, and so to bring good to the world around us.

Practices are the earthy business of encountering ideas, then working out how they might take shape in us. They help us move from aspiration to reality. They work slowly over time. We shouldn't expect immediate results, but we can be expectant that through them the change for good that we seek will come, gradually forming something new within us.

The practices in *Running Over Rocks* are 'spiritual'. That is most definitely not to confine them to some esoteric or religious sphere, but rather to see them as embracing all of human life. To be spiritual is to be human. To be human is to be spiritual. These spiritual practices are not a ladder of achievement. They are not just for those who might be perceived as spiritually inclined, gifted or educated. They can't be ticked off as 'done'. They are about a daily choice to move in the directions that are good for us, good for the people around us, and good for the earth.

Ritual and Playful

Some of the practices have been crafted over centuries in contemplative and active traditions around the world. Others are only emerging in the twenty-first century as humans learn together how to negotiate the particular challenges of the present moment. And each one is rooted in my own experiments at becoming truly human, learning from the gift of those inspiring people whose path I have found myself stumbling onto – the saints and the mystics, the monastics and the contemplatives, the dreamers and the activists, the poets and the teachers, the artists and the musicians, the makers and the explorers in every area of human activity who have walked the path towards becoming truly human.

Many of the practices have a ritual quality to them. As human beings we have always formed rituals around what truly matters to us. This sense of ritual means that we approach a practice with care, with attention and even with love. As a ritual a practice is not just a pragmatic means to an end, like perhaps going on a crash diet striving for weight loss. Rather the ritual reveals a sense of wonder in the practice. So, for example, a ritual (and spiritual) approach to diet would not just be about losing weight but about enjoying the food we eat, loving our bodies, and honouring the earth that sustains us. This ritual approach opens us up to the tender and mysterious qualities of life. If ritual implies a sense of seriousness, we'll also discover that practices work well when we approach them with curiosity, and even with playfulness. Experiment with them, give them time, let them work on you!

The Digging of Wells, the Search for Water

Every spiritual path, tradition or religion that is rooted in love, shaped in compassion and lived with integrity offers its particular gift to the world. In this way many wells have been dug in the search for spiritual water, and water has been found, brought to the surface and shared. And the formation of the practices in this book owes much to insights drawn from traditions other than the one in which I have been most deeply shaped – and particularly from the contemplative and mystical wells within them.[2]

---

2 See, for example, learning from the wisdom and experience of Islamic Sufism and Zen Buddhism in Practice 5, 'Garden Eden' and Practice 26, 'Live with Momentum'.

There is one well on which the book draws most deeply. The particular gift of Christianity – the well of my own experience – is Jesus the Christ,[3] the first-century Jewish teacher and healer whose life and teaching has had an extraordinary impact around the world. *Running Over Rocks* is dug deep into what I describe as the *ancient and unfolding Jesus tradition*. This is the ancient tradition in which I have been formed and the unfolding context in which I am attempting to live. It's also a tradition that I have found to be compelling. I've never been able to let it go, and it has never let go of me. Drawing from its mother tradition of Judaism, it is a flow of wisdom, energy and possibility that I sense may once again be experienced as a great gift to people of all spiritualities, all religions, all traditions, and to people who might claim no such path – a deep well for all our thirsts.[4]

The Ancient and Unfolding Jesus Tradition

In human terms the well of the Jesus tradition is relatively *ancient*. It has been drawn from and sustained lives around the world for almost two thousand years – and within the roots of the Jewish faith for centuries before that. In the wider story of the cosmos, of course, the telling of the story is very new indeed, but at its best the Jesus tradition has always carried a serious sense of setting within and engagement with the truly ancient story of the cosmos. The tradition is also *unfolding*, in the sense that it is always being lived out in new contexts. So to live the tradition is an experience of making friends both with irresistible old truths (to find ourselves saying 'Of course!') and with joyful new surprises ('Wow!').

---

3 'The Christ' is a title that in Greek means 'the anointed one', a translation of the Hebrew word 'Messiah', which carries a sense of this person being the One chosen and promised to bring salvation.

4 There's a fascinating story in the Gospel of John (chapter 4) in which an unnamed Samaritan woman shares water and conversation with Jesus at a well, during which he says, 'those who drink of the water that I will give them will never be thirsty'.

The practices in *Running Over Rocks* are given particular shape by the Gospels, the Parables and the Beatitudes – the stories surrounding Jesus, and his own enigmatic stories and sayings. St Mark, the writer of what was probably the first of the Gospels, memorably opens his account of the life of Jesus by describing the story that will unfold as 'good news'[5] for the hearer. And the writer of the last of the Gospels, St John, pictures Jesus as 'the light of all people'.[6] Perhaps this tradition may become again *good news* for each one of us, *shining light* on what is happening all around us, illuminating hidden or long-forgotten wisdom for life, revealing what we already instinctively know is true in our own experience, helping us to articulate that experience, and opening up whatever we hope for but may not dare to name.

Towards a Life of Presence

Dig deeper into *Running Over Rocks* and you'll discover towards the end of the book a series of practices that have become core to the way that the Jesus tradition has been practised over two millennia. Through these practices a surprising possibility seems to emerge. Not only may we find wisdom for life in the teachings of Jesus, but what I'll call the possibility of moving from *absence towards presence*. We may discover how to become more truly present to ourselves and to the world around us. We may also find ourselves encountering the astounding possibility of sacred presence, discovering that we are not alone, but deeply connected and held, loved and danced-with, delightful and gazed-upon – that the divine is somehow close to us, *with* us, even *within* us.

The ancient Jesus tradition is a mix of learning, wisdom and practice that may surprise those of us who live in the so-called developed West. It has (Middle) Eastern roots. It's as much about

---

5 Mark 1.1a: 'The beginning of the good news of Jesus Christ'.

6 John 1.4: 'What has come into being in him was life, and the life was the light of all people.'

being as doing. It is grounded in self-awareness. It is messy and delightful. And it takes shape in practice. Whatever your own experiences of spirituality, faith or religion, I hope that you will find yourself drawn towards one or more of these ancient practices, and perhaps discover something here that may give you joy, clarity and inspiration to keep on exploring the gift of your path. The Jesus tradition is a shimmering light of stillness, authenticity and hope, sometimes barely discernible but always present in the storm of words and images that form the backdrop to our lives. I hope that this book will inspire you to look deeper for signs of its shining, and to allow that light to illuminate the way ahead for you.

Movement From Towards

The practices in *Running Over Rocks* take shape in key areas of human experience. Every practice is a *movement away from* the many destructive and despairing ways of being with which we can find ourselves colluding, and a *movement towards* the more creative and hopeful ways that are already present within us, waiting to be (re)encountered and lived:

Practices of Earth and Body (from separation towards belonging)
Practices of Stillness and Movement (from complexity towards simplicity)
Practices of Descent (from anxiety towards acceptance)
Practices of Ascent (from scarcity towards abundance)
Practices of Possibility (from loss towards grace)
Practices of Peace (from despondency towards transformation)
Practices of the Beloved Life (from absence towards presence)
Practices of Love (from fear towards love)

The rocks of disturbance are often best negotiated in the company of others, so the book includes reflections on the importance of relationship and community. But the main focus is on discovering life practices that can be initiated by you, on your own, as you are, in your own context. Running over rocks has to start here and now, wherever we are!

Engaging with *Running Over Rocks*: From Poem to Practice

There are various ways to engage with this book. You can read it through, cover to cover. I hope you will. Fifty-two chapters follow the Introduction, each offering a practice for bringing goodness to the world, so you could experiment with a new practice each week of the year. The main part of the book is also divided up into seven series of seven practices – so you could work with a series for a season of the year, or for a season in your life, perhaps with friends. I have suggested how each series may link particularly well with a season of the Church year – the cycle that reflects on the extraordinary life of Jesus.

Running through the core of the book are fifty-three new poems. Each chapter begins with one, and whenever I do events around themes of spiritual practice the poems are invariably the starting point of our musing together. You might like to let the poems work away in you, and keep returning to them. I'd love you to do that. A poem doesn't attempt to tell the whole story, but to hint and suggest, to ignite the imagination, inviting you as reader or hearer to bring your own experience and intuition to the conversation. The spaciousness of a poem is a gift that enables us to discover for ourselves the possibilities that are already within us.

Tough times threaten to destabilize us, throwing us off course and tempting us to abandon our search for the good path that we once sensed was waiting for us, a path on which we may even have set out, but perhaps have now left behind or forgotten. How easily we lose our attention, our focus, and our open-heartedness. How rapidly we lose our clarity, our transparency, and our light. This is perhaps what Jesus had in mind when he said that to rediscover the goodness within ourselves and to bring blessing to the world we need to become 'pure in heart'. Becoming pure in heart is the work of becoming truly human. It is demanding, but necessary, and full of delight. So I invite you to explore with me. Together may we find a path towards the life that awaits us.

May we live again with imagination, adventure and generosity
May we bring goodness to the world around us
May we learn to be truly, fully, joyfully human
May we rediscover our purity of heart
May we run over rocks . . .

PRACTICES OF EARTH AND BODY

From separation towards belonging: re-learning to live as human beings in the world

Connecting with an ancient standing stone on the north coast of the Isle of Mull.

We are the ash-dust of ancient stars. We are earth. We are water. *We are body*. We are also amazing centres of curious consciousness. We are thinkers and makers, wonderers and questioners. *We are mind*. And we are something perhaps harder to define but brilliantly vibrant. We are the burning light within us, dancing with the shimmering light around us. We are grace. We are soul. *We are spirit*.

We seem to easily forget as human beings that we are body, mind and spirit, that each element is vital to our well-being, and that each is deeply connected to the other. So how might we bring these elements within us together? This first series of practices offers a path to help us to come home to ourselves through a rediscovery of our own physicality, and of our place in the natural world. Many of us have become disconnected from our own bodies and from the earth that is our home. We need to learn to walk again as human beings on the earth, to be at

1

ease with ourselves and to be at one with the earth from which we have come and to which our bodies will return.

Seasons connected with these Practices of Earth and Body are Advent and the Nativity. These seasons celebrate the divine taking earthy form in Jesus of Nazareth, who becomes body, mind and spirit as one of us, with us and for us.

1

Come Home to Your Body

SKINNYDIPPER

From a trail of blue clothes
flung onto sand you
walked into the sea, deep and strong,
seeking your hiddenness
scouring your fears
salting your dreams.
You lifted your arms, throwing off
whatever you carried here, to embrace
whatever awaited you, this sacred place.

Three times you immersed yourself,
an Atlantic baptism in ancient water
in far-travelled sunlight
and in oyster catcher's cry
waiting for this moment
this revelation, this small Eden.

Skinnydipper, naked in the naked sea
returning to your child, to your woman
to your goddess, your body singing
you threw back your head laughing.
Come on in, you said
come on in . . .

A woman stood behind Jesus at his feet, weeping, and began to bathe his feet with her tears and to dry them with her hair. Then she continued kissing his feet and anointing them with the ointment.

From the life of Jesus: Luke 7.38

Coming Home

All you need is a stretch of deserted beach, lake, loch or river. Perhaps the sun breaking through. A desire to reconnect. And the impulsive courage to slip into the wildness of water. The spiritual life is not an ethereal, other-worldly thing, but a gritty, earthy, human endeavour. To live a spiritual life is to discover a way of being that encompasses all that we are as human beings, connecting our inner person and our outer life, reflecting our best aspirations and our less-than-perfect realities. Our inner spark takes shape in the earthy reality of human bodies in engagement with the world around us. We need to *come home to our bodies.*

We have a complicated relationship with our bodies. They are the *us* that we see in the mirror and they are the first *us* that others see when they encounter us. We know that our bodies are part of *us* and yet we are tempted to see them as separate from 'us'. So we say, for example, 'My head is hurting me'. Most of us have some kind of issues with our bodies. If only I was thinner. Or more muscled. If only I was less ungainly. Or more beautiful. So we can end up feeling disconnected from our bodies, let down by them, and sometimes even ashamed of them to the point where we hide them or hide from them. The first practice in *Running Over Rocks* is to discover something that enables you to come home to your body.

Dust and Tears

Some religious traditions, Christianity certainly included, have played a contributory role in spreading a mistrust of the human body.[1] But Jesus himself seems to have allowed himself to be encountered in remarkably embodied ways. Perhaps this is not so surprising. He is, after all, grounded in the story of beginnings told in the Jewish scriptures, in which God 'formed man from the dust of the ground, and breathed into his nostrils the breath of life; and the man became a living being'.[2] Earthy stuff.

I love one of the more scandalous stories told about Jesus, recorded in the Gospel of Luke.[3] A woman with some kind of bad reputation finds out that he is being entertained at the home of a Pharisee – a religious leader. She crashes the dinner, goes to where Jesus is reclining and begins to wash his feet 'with her tears'. She then dries them with her hair, kisses them, and anoints them with expensive perfume. Even in a culture where foot-washing was an accepted part of hospitality this is an intimate connection to the body, and Jesus' acceptance of the woman's touch, tears and kisses is treated as outrageous by the host. Jesus, however, seems to be very happy with the woman's physical touch. His response suggests that our inner life (and, in the case of this woman, perhaps her gratitude to Jesus for seeing in her the goodness that others miss) needs to find expression in our physical bodies. It just doesn't work to live away from our bodies. We need to come home.

---

1 The way that the writings of St Paul have been sometimes (mis)used is an obvious example from within the Christian tradition. But as a teacher of Jewish faith-practice Paul would have been aware of both the sanctity of the human body and its celebration in Jewish life.

2 Genesis 2.7.

3 Luke 7.36–50. There's a similar story in John's Gospel 12.1–8.

Unexpected Euphoria

The morning bell[4] has been rung. A candle is lit by the icon. A line from the Gospels read, repeated, then let go, into stillness. Now, standing, some warm-up bends. Into a series of sun salutations. Then, down into a slow movement between cat and child, long breaths, attentive pauses. Sit in that lovely twist. On our backs now, another stretching posture with legs and head falling away from each other in time with our breathing. Unexpected euphoria! Then into a foetal position, long stretches and wide circles. Keep breathing deep. Roll like baby. Onto the stomach. Flying. Into sphinx, that sweet releasing curve in the spine. Walking to our feet with our hands. Into a series of warrior asanas. Tree balance. Then into our prayer stances. But were we not praying before? Of course we were. The movement carries our prayer. The movement is our prayer.

Through a simple practice of yoga, much of it learned during our experiments in contemplative spirituality in the StillPoint[5] project, I've been able to re-encounter my body, and to recover a sense of my body's natural movement.[6] Of course I'm a long way from recovering the flexibility that I had as a child running over rocks, but I feel much more at one with my body than I have done for a very long time. And it has been a revelation to experience how yoga as recovery of natural body movement can come together so beautifully with other practices of a contemplative life in the ancient and unfolding Jesus tradition (which we'll explore later in the book) – reading the great texts, prayer of words, prayer with icons and stillness.

---

4 Morning bell: a daily way into prayer – www.belovedlife.org.
5 www.thestillpoint.org.uk.
6 Thanks to our yoga teacher James Jewell for this insight: www.jamesjewell.info.

Come Home to Your Body: A Practice

 For the practice of *Come Home to Your Body* I invite you to look for something that will enable your body to open up, to breathe deep, and to unfurl. Let yourself be drawn to something that is (or could become) somehow natural to you – perhaps walking or running, swimming or dancing, some simple stretching or yoga. This practice is not about pushing your body, dominating it or breaking through some kind of barrier.[7] This is about loving your body, respecting its giftedness, and coming home to yourself. It's important with this and with all the practices in *Running Over Rocks* to nurture something that can become part of your rhythm of life. Best to do a little and often, ideally every day. Whatever you choose, do it with loving attention. It can be really helpful to do this practice with someone else. It has helped me to have a daily yoga partner. Some mornings one or the other of us will need the shared commitment to turn up. Or the mats will remain furled, and us with them.

---

7 If you have any doubt at all about your physical ability to take something up make sure that you get some expert advice.

2

Walk the Good Earth

SKIMMING STONES

Settling in my palm is a bleached pebble
bearing sacred imprint of its improbable
making. I press it tumbled-smooth
to my lips, roll it depth-cold on my face
then find it turning slowly in my hand
an ocean rosary for my prayers
each rotation drawing me into the beginning
and on to the ending of everything. Time

now to conspire in its unlikely flight
to wonder at its brief dance in bright light
with wave, with earth and with tide –
each splash an awakening
from all I knew of stone and air,
of weight and water, of falling and rising.
I follow its shining path, its track of glory
into its disappearing.

*Crowds would gather to hear Jesus and to be cured of their
diseases. But he would withdraw to deserted places and pray.*

From the life of Jesus: Luke 5.15b–16

Earth-People

It is 4pm on a cold afternoon in south Devon. I've been working all day and it's time for a walk. It's my fourth winter here and the local patterns of tide, wind and cloud are becoming more familiar. There's perhaps an hour before a cold rain will come in from the north west. The hill tops and crags of the great Dartmoor will still be visible if I leave now. This is a day for boots, for an extra top layer, for gloves and for a hat to shield my ears from the wind.

There are many and undoubted benefits in the way we live now, but we have paid a heavy price for them. One of the costliest losses has been our widespread disconnection from the earth that nurtures us and from the creatures and life forms that share the planet with us. Very few of us do our work in the natural landscape, and we can easily forget our connection to it. We've lost something vital here. We are *Earth-People*, and to forget where we come from damages us, and it damages the earth. We are part of a wider pattern of existence. If we neglect our connection to the natural world we will lose our bearings in the unfolding story of the earth – and that is a dangerous loss, for us and for the planet.

Of course very few people would either want or be able to return to a simple subsistence-farming existence. We cannot turn back the clock on the growth of human population or the nature of human development. But we can and must take our place again in companionship with the astonishing blue-green planet in a spirit of humility, love and ingenuity. Whenever we engage in practices that remind us that we are Earth-People we will rediscover who we are and connect more deeply into the nature and mystery of existence itself, its patterns of flowering and fading, of death-seed and resurrection-shoot.

Blessed are the Earthy

We know that Jesus walked his landscape. And this, it seems to me, was not just through necessity. The sayings and stories of Jesus reveal how much he loved the landscape in which he walked, how he gave it close attention, and how much he was formed by it. The northern hills of Israel and the deserts of Judea, the 'deserted places', are his preferred locations for prayer, his places of retreat and restoration, reflection and thanksgiving, questioning and re-imagining. On the hillsides that enfold the Sea of Galilee he sits to teach the crowds who follow him. The fields and the tracks that cross these hills produce the earthy background for his parables. The region's weather patterns and the seasons' turnings shape his sense of what may be emerging. And the local birds and animals keep on surfacing in his stories, icons of God's love.

'Blessed are the earthy' was not one of Jesus' sayings, but I'll contend for it as being in the spirit of his teachings. By his life and teaching he encourages human connection with the soil, envisages people in tune with their landscape, and imagines a future where humans live once again as friends and lovers with and within the great earth-garden.

The Wild Forest in Your Street

Reconnection to the earth must start close to home. One of the greatest gifts we may be able to give to our children and their children is a simple experience of the natural world. And this doesn't need to be an expensive visit to the Alps, the Polar ice-cap or the Amazonian rainforest. In fact it must involve reconnection *wherever we are*. And as we nurture a deeper sense of connection something interesting happens: if we can connect with our small local part of the earth we can begin to connect with it all. Begin to do this and you may discover that the earth's wild forests are waiting to be encountered in the woods at the end of your street.

That the great rivers of the world are flowing in the stream that meanders through your local park. And that the planet's rarest wild flowers are breaking through the concrete in the pavement outside your house.

A Maori friend told me once of her sense of belonging to her home-place in New Zealand. We belong, she told me, to this mountain. How interesting that she didn't say that the mountain belonged to her or to her people. We belong, she said, to this mountain. So may we discover that we too, wherever we are, belong to this mountain, to these trees, to this stream, to these flowers, to this street, to this neighbourhood – and to the whole earth.

Walk the Good Earth: A Practice

 I call this practice *Walk the Good Earth*. You may prefer to *run* the good earth, or *cycle* the good earth. You might only be able to *sit* on the good earth. Whatever your preference, the core of the practice is the same: to discover a way to be with the earth. To be out in the natural world. To find your place in the landscape. To enter again into local relationship with the planet and its creatures. We need to walk the earth to rediscover our place in it. And, incidentally, until we walk the earth all the debates and statistics about the state of the environment are likely to remain as theories. In the act of walking we are close to the ground. The earth can engage with us. If we do this often enough we may discover that the landscape will open up its life to us, inspiring us to become more fully and beautifully human. So, what might be the walk in the company of the good earth that you could take today? Where will you go?

3

Close-up (Terra Divina)

IN THE HOLLOW OF A BLADE OF GRASS

Put down your iPad
and put on your boots
let's walk for a mile
we'll cross that stile
and follow the sloping path
up Bigbury hill.

We'll fall to the ground
and lie face down, laughing
children again of the red soil,
enchanted. And cradled
in the hollow of a blade of grass
we may find the ancient life of the universe
dancing still in
one clear
drop of
last
night's
rain.

And why do you worry about clothing? Consider the lilies of the field, how they grow; they neither toil nor spin, yet I tell you, even Solomon in all his glory was not clothed like one of these.

A teaching of Jesus: Matthew 6.28–29

The Secret of the Universe

There's a tiny coral-coloured flower at the field's edge on Drunkard's Hill. Perhaps only 5mm across at its widest, it's easy to miss as it hugs the ground. But this small flower may contain the secrets of the universe.

'Consider the lilies of the field', said Jesus.[1] It's interesting to note the context in which he suggests this botanical adventure. It's about worrying – or to be precise it's about not worrying.[2] Jesus teaches that if we can learn to give close attention to the natural world around us a new way of seeing all of life may emerge. We'll get a new perspective. This process begins physically (simply but amazingly) – by getting out in the natural world. When we do this our bodies recover their balance. This in itself is good for us. We are body, mind and spirit, and our bodies need releasing. A journey into the landscape can do this.

But the life of the landscape itself may also offer the possibility of a shift in perspective. The natural world comes full of gift, offering wisdom and insight. An unexpected solution to a problem can open up as we pause by a stream. Clarity over a future direction might reveal itself as we make the choice to take a different pathway home. It's encouraging to see signs of renewed interest within the Jesus tradition in engaging with the wisdom of the earth. In the UK the small but growing Forest Church movement aims 'to learn, worship, meditate, pray and practise with the trees, at the spring, along the shore.'[3]

Twitching with Fragile Life

This re-visioning may further widen out and open up the very nature of existence. It reveals what we might call truth. This truth

---

1 Matthew 6.28.

2 Matthew 6.27–28.

3 www.mysticchrist.co.uk/forest_church.

may of course be mysterious. If you hadn't learned about it at school, how could you imagine what could become of a caterpillar? The change from one soft lively form into a hard lifeless box, and then the emergence of a seemingly new creature twitching with fragile life, about to fly. Astonishing universal truth displayed in tiny fluttering wings.

The natural world is not all great beauty, of course. The woods are full of death and dying, the seas surge with sorrow and loss, the skies can be heavy with darkening and falling. We'll ponder more on those processes later in the book but suffice to say here that close attention to the natural world reveals truth. In *Cave Refectory Road*[4] I suggested a way to the practice of Lectio Divina[5] with the great text of the natural world. I want to develop that idea further here. I call this practice *Close-up (Terra Divina).*[6] This may inspire you to fall to the ground and pay very close attention to a flower. It could also mean giving attention to a huge mountain landscape, letting the scale do its work on you. Either way, both ways, the natural world is full of truth.

Terra Divina

The practice of *Close-up (Terra Divina)* is in four steps:

Step one is *lectio*. This is reading the text of the landscape. Like reading a book, except now it's another language that you are reading – of clouds and birds and trees and sunlight. Here we are beginning to open ourselves up to the truth, wisdom, or gift that

---

4 Ian Adams, *Cave Refectory Road: Monastic rhythms for contemporary living*, London: Canterbury Press, 2010, pp. 55–8.

5 Lectio Divina is an ancient method nurtured by the Christian monastics to engage with the great written texts of the faith. They believed that the Scriptures have a living, breathing quality for the reader or hearer, whenever and wherever those texts are read or heard. Lectio Divina, literally 'sacred reading', is a way of allowing the text to speak now and always, in our context, in our time.

6 *Terra* in Latin means earth, land or soil.

the landscape may be offering us. Let's imagine you are going for a walk in the woods. You are beginning to create space for something to catch your attention. You become aware of the various sensations you feel, noticing the places where your attention lingers. Perhaps there's a breeze, and you notice that your attention keeps coming back to the sound and the motion of the leaves on the trees. This, you sense, may be a gift to you – although you don't know why.

Step two is *meditatio*. This is meditation, the stage where the mind is most active. Here we begin to wonder why whatever has caught our attention might have done so, and why it might be a gift to us. The gift may be a difficult one, but we can trust that in time it may indeed become a gift. The leaves have caught your attention. You notice that most of the leaves are not breaking off, but are held by branches which themselves are swaying, taking the shock of the wind into themselves. Perhaps the truth or gift here is that you too are being held.

Step three is *oratio*. This is prayer or yearning. Here we let the natural world work within us. So now let whatever has caught your attention (the physical sight, sound or sensation – not your thoughts about it) carry your prayers or yearnings. As things come to mind you let them be carried by the simple presence of this element of the natural world. So you let the sight and sound (or later in the day the *memory* of the sight and sound) of the branches absorbing the destructive power of the wind, absorb the destructive power of whatever is concerning you.

Step four is *contemplatio*. This is contemplation or presence. This can be like stepping into warm sunlight. It can also feel like nothing. In my experience both sensations are normal and good. Here you let go of whatever has caught your attention, and enjoy the sense of being alive, of being held, of being at one with everything. Some experience this as being held in a benevolent universe. In the ancient Jesus tradition this is understood as being in the presence of the community of God, the Holy Trinity. So now you close your eyes and let the sound of the wind in the leaves and the sensation of the breeze on your face work within you. After a few minutes there may be a hint that, as the great English mystic Mother Julian of Norwich discovered through her own practice of earth divina,[7] 'all will be well and all manner of things will be well'.

Close-up (Terra Divina): A Practice

 As you engage in your practice of *Walk the Good Earth* experiment with the four steps of *Close-up (Terra Divina)*. Here they are in short-form:

Let your attention be caught. This may be a gift.
Ask yourself: what has caught my attention – and why might this be a gift?
Allow whatever has caught your attention to carry your prayers or yearnings.
Finally, let go of whatever has caught your attention, and enjoy the possibility of sacred presence.

---

7 Julian of Norwich famously discovered that everything exists because it is loved by God as she held a little thing 'the size of a hazelnut'.

4

Keep Festival (Live the Season)

THE WISDOM OF ROCKS

On Porthmeor
today at far low tide
I pressed my lips to the sun-warmed skin
of an oil-black rock, each plane
and crease a vein
of wisdom millions of years
in the shaping.

The rock whispered to me:
every tide can be trusted
every storm brings a gift
every shaft of light gives
a glimpse of what truly is.

Again I pressed my lips to the sun-warmed skin
and whispered to the rock:
tell me more . . .

When it is evening, you say, 'It will be fair weather, for the sky is red.' And in the morning, 'It will be stormy today, for the sky is red and threatening.' You know how to interpret the appearance of the sky, but you cannot interpret the signs of the times.

A teaching of Jesus: Matthew 16.2–3

A Month's Rain in a Day

The month of May in England. Everything is full of promise. The trees are suddenly in full canopy. On the radio and in the fields Ralph Vaughan-Williams' lark is ascending. And if we are so blessed, there may be some warm days, and an occasional pint in the pub garden by a meandering river. But of course May doesn't always turn out quite as we had imagined – and the earth is currently experiencing some new, not always welcome, variations to seasonal weather. Nevertheless the bigger picture of seasonal change rolls on.

The patterns of the seasons' passing, turning and coming teach us about waiting for the hoped-for-but-unseen thing to happen. They teach us to persist, to yearn and to imagine. They show us that things have to die for new life to emerge. And the vagaries of seasonal weather and their unexpected events tell us that everything going perfectly in life is not natural. The late frost, the early snowstorm and the month's rain in a day remind us that life comes with surprise. This is how life is, and it's not a good idea to try to control it. Rather, we need to give attention to how we respond to the weather patterns that come in.

Summer Turned to High

The unstoppable nature of the seasons makes clear that there is a bigger picture than our own concerns. We can become so focused on the detail of our own lives that we lose sight of the wider patterns of which we are (amazingly, mysteriously) a part. Patterns of change and growth, of rising and falling, of greeting and farewell. We can't hold onto May for ever. And actually, as lovely as May can sometimes be in northern Europe, we know instinctively that it will be good to welcome June and the coming of summer (we hope) turned to high. The seasons' journeys remind us of our own need to move lovingly through the seasons of life.

If we allow ourselves to re-enter the story that the seasons tell we will find ourselves drawn into a wider appreciation of growth and maturity. We may begin to truly live the seasons of life as gifts. It's great to be 20 or 50 or 80 years old. But 21, 51 and 81 will need embracing, loving and living. The next phase of our working life may discover a new shape. Our relationships may evolve into something more mature. The years of old age may begin to open up with a new sense of possibility. The earth cares for itself and for us, and each season of the earth is full of love. Similarly each season of life holds within it the seeds of love, if only we can let those seeds come to fruit within us. So how can we do this?

We seem to have lost much of the old wisdom of the seasons – wisdom that would have been very familiar to our ancestors. There are interesting signs that some in the Jesus tradition in the British Isles are beginning to rediscover the wisdom of the seasons, learning in part from other spiritual traditions which have kept their interest in this alive. The 'Communities of the Mystic Christ'[1] project has a particular interest in the seasons of the year, their meaning and gift. Wisdom and practice emerging around the patterns of equinox and solstice, fire festival and solar season, earth preparation and harvest were once vital here. For our well-being as humans and for the good of the earth it may be important that they become so again. The project is discovering how the festivals of the Jesus tradition flow within and alongside these seasonal celebrations, offering their complementary wisdom for the season.

Changing Seasons, Changing World

Jesus tried to get people to make the link between the seasons of the year and the seasons of life. You are good at observing the weather, he tells his hearers, but you fail to see the signs of change in your own lives, in your society, in your culture. In the Gospel accounts

1 www.mysticchrist.co.uk: 'Exploring a journey in community with the Mystic Christ towards personal transformation and the renewal of creation.'

of the last year of his life we find a Jesus who is very conscious of
the changing seasons of his life. He is both aware and accepting
of the heavy weather – the suspicion, rejection and persecution
– that is sweeping in for him. The Son of Man, he says ('Child of
Humanity' we might say – and a favourite saying used by Jesus to
describe himself) is destined to face insults, beatings and death.[2]
Jesus embodies a wise acceptance of the seasonal nature of life.

So the practice of *Keep Festival (Live the Season)* is about embracing the seasons and their changing. This is perhaps the first of
the practices in *Running Over Rocks* that could be described as a
stance. By this I mean a chosen way of thinking, feeling and acting
– a way of being that seeps into everything that we are and everything that we do. It's about making a choice to live in the season
that you are now in, and being ready to welcome the new season
that is coming. It's about the physical seasons of the earth as it
spins through cosmos and time. And it's about our own seasons of
life. The way we engage with the earth season can help shape how
we engage with whatever the oncoming season of life that we face
might bring to us.

Keep Festival (Live the Season): A Practice

The stance of *Keep Festival (Live the Season)* begins
with our attitude to the earth's seasons. If we can
enter winter with joy we'll have a chance of navi-
gating *life's* winter seasons well. A way into this is
simply to do the things that the season seems to
call for. To truly mark, celebrate and live the season. So when
summer comes (yes, often all too briefly in this part of the world),
if you can, eat outside sometimes. When the autumn storms arrive,
get out in the rain and feel it on your skin. When the cold of winter
arrives, take joy in making a fire. When spring shows its face, begin

---

2 Luke 18.32–33.

something new, a way for you to echo the emergence of new life from a dormant landscape.

A further step into this practice is to begin to (re)discover the old earth-season wisdom where you are. Explore how the seasons may have been marked here in the past – and imagine how they might be celebrated again now. And so together, let's *Keep Festival*, and *Live the Season*!

5

Garden Eden

THE EARTH WILL HEAL ITSELF

when we are gone
the earth will heal itself
when we are gone
the air will breathe deep again
when we are gone
the clouds will carry their spring rain
when we are gone
the concrete will crumble to its core
when we are gone
the plastic will return to its source
when we are gone
the estuary will drink from the sea
when we are gone
the bees will nurture new colonies
when we are gone
the road will flower into a meadow
when we are gone
the tuna will leap with joy
when we are gone
the glass will grain into sand
when we are gone
the sun will warm new life and
when we are gone
the earth will heal itself
when we are gone

The kingdom of God is as if someone would scatter seed on the ground, and would sleep and rise night and day, and the seed would sprout and grow, he does not know how. The earth produces of itself . . .

A teaching of Jesus: Mark 4.26–28a

The Quest of the Blueberry Plant

There's a blueberry plant outside our back door, a gift from friends. It's rarely impressive. For many months of the year it's bare and the crop is not abundant. But I love it. As in other areas of engagement with the natural world, many of us have lost the need, desire or ability to grow food. We are all a little poorer for this. Growing plants and caring for animals highlights our interconnectedness and belonging among all that exists. We humans have often imagined and acted as if everything else in the world is there simply to enable us to do our thing. We have placed ourselves at the centre of everything. As if it's all about us! But the truth is that we are just a part (though at our best an amazing part) of a much bigger (and even more amazing) picture. Part of all that exists. So can we find our true place of belonging once more? Can we become ourselves? Can we *Garden Eden*?[1]

This is part of a compelling strand of thinking that has emerged in the mystical streams of some of the great religions and spiritual paths – the idea that everything is entrusted with being truly itself. So the blueberry plant at our back door is on a quest. It has accepted its calling to be a blueberry plant. Its life cycle is focused on producing a small crop of blueberries. It puts up with the vagaries of the British weather, copes with the attention of insects, and lives with the indignity of being relatively naked for six months of the year. So that it can be a blueberry plant, bringing a small amount

---

1 Eden is the paradise setting for humanity in the ancient story of beginnings in Genesis (2.8).

of joy to the insects who live on it, the one who tends it, his family and any visitors who come during the brief season of scarce fruit. In its simplicity and humility, it shines.

Remembering Who We Are

We might say that it's only we humans who have lost our way. Could it be that we alone as a species have forgotten to be who we are? We have dehumanized ourselves so often and in so many ways. In the terms of the essence of the ancient Jewish scriptures, as taught by the rabbi Jesus, we have forgotten our calling to love God and love neighbour.[2] And in 'neighbour' we can include the planet and all its creatures.

So can we remember who we are? And can we once again become good neighbours? The often unrecognized longing to re-discover our calling to be fully human in the same spirit as the rest of the natural world is expressed, by the thirteenth-century mystic and Sufi poet Rumi, as a desire to rediscover our voice:

Birdsong brings comfort
to my longing
I'm just as ecstatic as they are,
but with nothing to say!
Please universal soul, practise
some song or something through me!

Can we become as fully, ecstatically human as the singing bird is fully, ecstatically bird? Recovering a sense of what it means to be a graceful humanity within a wider world of grace will take time. We will need to grow into that memory again. And being involved in the very earthy matter of trying to grow something may help us do this. It takes us immediately into the pattern, heartache and

---

2 Matthew 22.34–40.

gift of slowness. You can't hurry growth. As Jesus pointed out, we can plant and tend the crop but its growth is a mystery beyond our control. *The earth produces of itself.* We can do our bit but the growth is actually beyond us. And so in the greater mystery that is life, growth will happen (or not happen) in us, around us, and even despite us. This sense of our own limitation is a really useful lesson for all of life. We cannot control what comes our way. We can prepare the ground, we can work to reduce dangers, we can shape the environment, but then something more mysterious comes into play.

Digging with the Diggers

Drawing on his experience of living in an economy with a heavy reliance on local agriculture and fishing, Jesus drew on themes of growing and harvesting to let his stories make their points and ask their questions. There's a sense within his teachings that the soil is sacred – and our engagement with it should be revered. This was one of the sources of inspiration for the Diggers (or True Levellers as they called themselves),[3] a movement of radical land-reforming Protestants who planted up some common ground on George Hill in Surrey in 1649, in the wake of the first English[4] Civil War. This is from the Digger manifesto, 'Levellers Standard Advanced'.[5]

> In that we begin to Digge upon George-Hill, to eate our Bread together by righteous labour, and sweat of our browes, It was shewed us by Vision in Dreams, and out of Dreams, That that should be the Place we should begin upon; And though that Earth in view of Flesh, be very barren, yet we should trust the

---

3 Diggers was a name given to the group by their opponents.

4 The repercussions of the Civil War were not confined to England but were felt – sometimes brutally – right across the United Kingdom and Ireland.

5 *Levellers Standard Advanced or The State of Community Opened, and Presented to the Sons of Men*, April 1649.

Spirit for a blessing . . . taking the Earth to be a Common Treasury, as it was first made for all.

Perhaps the time has come again for the righteous labour of working the soil, and for trusting the fecund Spirit to bless us and whatever we are involved in growing. This practice I am calling *Garden Eden*. It's simple enough, and not at all dependent on having a garden. (We ourselves have only a small courtyard.) You can grow plants on a window sill. Or you could do some 'guerrilla gardening', planting flowers in neglected or unloved public spaces – a sign perhaps of what Jesus referred to as the kingdom of heaven or the kingdom of God being all around us.

Garden Eden: A Practice

 Do some research, get yourself to a local garden centre or farm shop, and let yourself be drawn to a plant that you'd like to grow, for food or for beauty. You could begin with seeds or with seedlings. Enjoy the plant becoming itself. See how the experience begins to flow into other areas of your life, gently reshaping you as a human being, remembering who you are, reminding you of the wider world of which you are part. Grow something. Give the process your deep attention. *Garden Eden* and see what begins to change.

6

Kitchen Jazz

CULLEN SKINK

Handle with tenderness
season with intuition
heat with attention
separate with devotion
unearth with anticipation
cut with precision
slice with tears
pour with thankfulness
serve with abundance.

And so reverence the silvered fish
and her companions
with your love.

When (Simon Peter, Thomas called the Twin, Nathanael of Cana in Galilee, the sons of Zebedee, and two others of his disciples) had gone ashore, they saw a charcoal fire there, with fish on it, and bread. Jesus said to them, 'Bring some of the fish that you have just caught.'

From the life of Jesus: John 21.9–10

Wonder of the Fish

I'm working on a south-west variation of cullen skink – the evoca-
tive name for a traditional fish soup from Scotland. The core ingredients are smoked fish, potatoes, onions and leeks, water and milk.
I'm experimenting with different fish, with the degree of mashing,
and with a variety of herbs. The poem began to form one afternoon as I was preparing the ingredients for a cullen skink that
evening. The words began to shape themselves like a simple litany,
a prayer, even an act of devotion. The task helped form the words,
the words helped shape the task.

The task of preparing food is a daily opportunity to reconnect
with the earth. And we have a choice. We can prepare food to make
a meal. Or we can prepare the food *to prepare the food*, with care
and attention to the ingredients, so that it in turn, at the right time,
may become a meal. There is a difference! There's something really
important about handling the ingredients for a meal with love, seeing the dignity, beauty and mystery of life in the humblest of its
forms. If I can see the wonder in a flake of fish, I can begin to see
wonder everywhere. The process of treating ingredients with love
is therefore also a step towards treating our fellow human beings
with the care and attention that they deserve. There is a caricature
around that the top chefs love their food but need to bawl at their
staff to get the job done. I hope this is a false picture. How we treat
our ingredients is a step towards how we treat the people around us.

The combining of ingredients, timings and seasonings offers
learning for life. Each herb and spice works in its own way to bring
out the flavour of a food or complement it. And the timing of the
cooking process can radically alter the taste the food for better or
for worse. Preparing a meal takes time. Fast food offers us a quick
hit (and I'm up for an occasional rush) but the healthiest way to
eat is usually found in taking a more leisurely and deliberate path.
Growing food can't be rushed, and in the same way its preparation
and its consumption are best taken at a gentle pace.

Come and Have Breakfast

There's a story told in the Gospel of John about a breakfast. It's one of the truly great stories surrounding Jesus, breaking down any barriers we might be tempted to put up between spirituality and everyday life. On the Sea of Tiberias in the early morning light the dazed disciples, who have been out fishing all night without success, don't recognize the man who has (rather cheekily we might say) shouted advice to them from the shore. But they do as he suggests and put their nets out on the other side of the boat from where they have been fishing. A huge number of fish – 153 says John – are caught. The disciples haul their catch onto the shore. Jesus has set up a charcoal fire, some fish are already being cooked, and bread is ready. So come, he says, and have breakfast.

The details are important, not because there is hidden meaning in them, but because the earthy task of preparing and sharing food matters. This simple breakfast, lovingly prepared, will change the world. The reconciling conversation that the risen Jesus initiates through the meal becomes one of the key foundations for the often glorious, frequently disappointing but always pregnant-with-possibility community that emerges after the ascension, seeking to follow the Jesus path, the thing we call Church.

Kitchen as Sanctuary

If you are the person who seems to create most of the meals in your house this suggestion may be treated with a wry smile, a belly-laugh or a few flying vegetables. But here goes: at its best there is a giftedness in creating food for people. The problems come when we assume that someone else in the house will always do this, when we don't get involved ourselves, and whenever we don't honour the process. So if you are not usually involved in preparing food may this be an encouragement to you to begin!

Kitchen Jazz is the simple practice of preparing food with care, attention and even love. A lovely old word for this is *reverence*. Each ingredient offers itself, asking you to be both respectful and intuitive in the way that you work with them. This is the jazz of the kitchen. We work with the recipe handed down (the tradition); and we seek to be ready to play our own line (the improvisation). Step into the responsibility of this task, launch into the freedom that opens up. If we approach the preparation of food with reverence, the kitchen may begin to be revealed as sacred space, as house of prayer, as sanctuary.

Kitchen Jazz: A Practice

 As you prepare the food for your next meal, reverence every ingredient. Honour, respect and enjoy each element of the meal. Let their sight, their texture, their consistency and their aroma come to you. Each one brings its gift to the meal. And when the preparation and cooking are done, enjoy the privilege of making the invitation to table, the 'come to breakfast' call. Reverence this moment too. Like that early morning meal on the beach some two millennia ago shared by a handful of people, the meal you prepare and the conversation it inspires may just play their part in changing the world.

7

Love the Manual Task

STACKING WOOD

Stacking wood?
come close at rest. So can there be any greater pleasure than
the stack. The block, the pattern, the   gap. The spinning earth
memories. The grain, the scent, the hue. The clump, the bark,
that breathes, humble and strong. Rings seasoning the seasons
Is there any greater pleasure than stacking wood? Making a wall

There was a landowner who planted a vineyard, put a fence
around it, dug a wine press in it, and built a watchtower.

A parable of Jesus: Matthew 21.33a

Feeding the Hungry Stove-Animal

It's early morning in winter, and still dark. But the hungry stove-
animal[1] is calling. From mid-September well into April my day
invariably begins with preparing to feed her. Our wood-burner is
made by a company in Shropshire, birth-place in England of the
Industrial Revolution. It's simple in design, solid, well-engineered.
And in this house, much loved. On the coldest nights we'll fill it
with logs and burn it very slowly to keep the house warm through
the long hours of darkness, but most days it's a new start. Clear

---

1 Jane Kenyon 1947–95.

the ash box. Carry in logs from the side of the house. Then lay the
fire. Fold some paper, roll some cardboard, create a pyre of small
sticks and logs. Add bigger logs on top. Finally, clean the glass
door. When I light the fire I sit in front of the stove and watch the
mystery flicker into being again. I'm entering into a very old ritual.

One aspect of our disconnection from the earth and from our
own bodies is the loss, for many of us, of our connection to manual
work. Of course few of us would welcome a life of tough manual
labour. And it's good that human ingenuity has meant that many
of the most repetitive, tough and dangerous tasks are now done by
machines. Preparing a few fish by hand can be enjoyable. Gutting
barrels of herring every day would be another matter. But perhaps
we've lost something if we rarely have the opportunity to engage
in a manual task, and to give the task our attention, our care, even
our devotion.

Ancient Blessings

Some manual tasks are, of course, easier to enjoy or more inspiring
than others. In the setting of a Devon village, tasks like stacking
wood and laying fires somehow feel right. They are long-performed
actions that tap into an older way of being human within the landscape. But who looks forward to putting out the refuse bins? But
then again, perhaps that's the point. I wonder if the putting out of
refuse bins could become a task that we do with more care and
attention – even if devotion might be a step too far? An archae-
ologist friend, one of whose specialities is the middens (refuse
heaps) of mesolithic people, tells me that there is plenty of evidence that these middens were created deliberately and carefully.
Discarded shells from those ancient shell-fish suppers weren't just
dropped anywhere.

The work done by the nineteenth-century folklorist Alexander
Carmichael in collecting details of the fast-disappearing oral tradition of the Highlands and Islands of Scotland is interesting in this

respect. Carmichael believed that many of the prayers, blessings, hymns and incantations that he heard might have been handed down unchanged from one generation to the next, as far back as the sixth century – the time of St Columba and other of the great Celtic saints. They reveal that these people honoured the manual work that had to be done, and created prayers and incantations for everyday manual tasks. Here's an excerpt from a blessing for the lighting of a fire in the morning:

> I will kindle my fire this morning
> In presence of the holy angels of heaven
> In presence of Ariel of the loveliest form,
> In presence of Uriel of the myriad charms
> Without malice, without jealousy, without envy,
> Without fear, without terror of any one under the sun,
> But the Holy Son of God to shield me.[2]

The repeated actions involved in laying up and lighting the day's fire become the setting for a blessing for the day, a prayer or mantra for how the fire-lighter will strive to live this day, conscious of the presence of the company of heaven, keeping the day's potential fears at bay.

Working the Land

The manual task done with care and attention represents our co-working with the great and amazing process of creating and sustaining. The wood stacked, the fire lit, the bins put out, are all part of a greater cycle of life into which we are invited to step. And we may be surprised to discover that when we give the manual task our attention something interesting can happen to our thought

---

2 'Beannachadh Beothachaid' (Blessing of the Kindling) from *Carmina Gadelica*, ed. C. J. Moore, Edinburgh: Floris Books, 1992.

process. A shift can occur, or an idea may emerge, as if from nowhere, that helps us work out how to handle an issue or take a step forward. Our physical movement, in engagement with a physical task, can somehow free up an internal movement, idea or possibility.

Working the land has long been both a motif for and a pathway into belonging. There can be something deeply satisfying about rediscovering our sense of being embodied through working with the landscape in which we are set. Jesus' parables are full of images of the manual task in the landscape. People plant vineyards, erect fences, and build towers. They plough fields, sow seeds, and harvest the crops. They make bread, graze sheep, and catch fish. Of course this is not surprising. At that time relatively few people made a living from words or ideas. The reality for the majority was some combination of craft and graft. The presence of these earthy images in the Jesus tradition connects him and us to the dignity of the manual task.

Love the Manual Task: A Practice

Love the Manual Task is about reconnecting ourselves with physical work. Like many of the practices in *Running Over Rocks*, this has its beginnings in the way we see things. Stacking wood, lighting the fire, or putting out the bins will just be more tasks to be finished as fast as possible unless we learn to see the worth, dignity and possibility in each task. So whatever the manual task that needs doing today, give it your attention. Sense the dignity of the task and the importance of doing it well. Allow the act to become a wordless prayer, entering into the earthy at-oneness of all things. Sense mind and body, task and thought coming together. And even receive the blessing of the task. Can there be any greater pleasure?

PRACTICES OF STILLNESS AND MOVEMENT

From complexity towards simplicity: discovering the essence

The clear sea at Traigh Ban Nam Monach (White Strand of the Monks) on Iona – a mesmerizing dance of sand, water and light.

We find much of our meaning and sense of self through our actions. Through the stuff we make, the actions we take, the things we do. That's natural, and fine as it goes. But instinctively most of us know that our true sense of identity may be found in a deeper place of stillness. We also sense that to venture in this direction will be at the same time both wonderful and disturbing. Stillness is one of the most demanding – and therefore least visited – places on the map of human existence. But it is full of promise.

It's not surprising then that many of us seem to have a predisposition towards action over stillness. Both impulses are vital, and they are connected, not opposites but companions. We need to discover how to form patterns of stillness and movement that nurture each other and help us to bring goodness to the world. This series of practices is aimed at helping us to find the deep connection between stillness and movement that will enable us to negotiate life as it comes – to run over rocks. A pattern of stillness and movement will help us to move from the damaging aspects of over-complication towards a mature and more simple approach to life, taking us closer to the essence of what it means to be truly human.

The season connected with these Practices of Stillness and Movement is Epiphany. In this season the ancient and unfolding Jesus tradition explores the possibility of enlightenment, of revelation of truth, and of what Orthodox theologians call theophany – the revealing of the divine. This is a season of mystery, of wonder, of revelation, of expanding horizon. Revelation often emerges in some experience of stillness. It then takes shape in movement as we act to bring good to the world.

8

Slow into Stillness

IN THIS STILLNESS

In this stillness
I discover so much noise.
Most of it is mine –
a box of jagged lines
a teeming tangle of connections
and disconnections, a snarl of anxieties
a barely-tethered storm fed
by fears and wounds I thought long bled dry.

But I need to remain here on this mat
to allow the noise to make its mark
and so in time to lose a little
of its power and intensity, to sense
the gaps appearing
clouds parting
spaces opening
for the quiet light to shine.

*Now during those days (Jesus) went out to the mountain to pray;
and he spent the night in prayer to God.*

From the life of Jesus: Luke 6.12

Do Nothing to Become Something

Do nothing. Do nothing to do something. Do nothing to become something.

Perhaps the most important movement we can ever make is, ironically, into stillness. To do something or to become something, it is necessary to do or to become (a kind of) nothing. Stillness is the starting point for much, perhaps even everything, that is truly good. In the great creation myth[1] of the Jewish scriptures the earth is spoken into being from stillness. A great wind begins to blow out of the darkness, and then God says 'Let there be light.' The word and the world are uttered out of silence. This is the tradition in which Jesus is formed. Inevitably we focus on his words and actions, but running through the Gospels we find at the heart of his practice a consistent commitment to stillness. He lives a pattern of withdrawal and engagement, of words and silence, of movement and ceasing, of gesture and pause – and if many of his actions take place in the busy towns, the quiet hills are his favoured setting for prayer.

The Vulnerability of Stillness

This practice emphasizes the importance of creating space for stillness. In stillness something interesting happens to us. Begin to practise stillness and you may start to find that much of whatever you thought was vital to you may in fact be relatively unimportant. This can be disorienting, and may account for why stillness, despite being longed for (notice how often we complain of being too busy!) seems to be so demanding. Stillness makes us feel vulnerable. It exposes our hidden priorities to the light. It shows us that much of our activity (however good, however important) is a frantic movement on the surface of something much deeper, qui-

---

1 Myth as meaning a story that contains deeper truth even than the literal account of an event.

eter, and more profound. We are like scurrying ants, pushing and shoving, carrying and manipulating the tasks that need to be done, ignoring the earth, strong and still beneath our scrambling feet.

But the demanding nature of stillness is also its gift. That painful sense of being opened up by stillness is what will free us. We can only re-orient ourselves towards whatever really matters by first encountering our false orientations, and by recognizing that if our sense of self-worth comes from what people think of us, or from what we achieve in life, we are likely to be disappointed. They may matter, but there is deeper truth.

Into an Unknown Land

Stillness is largely unmapped territory. The sixteenth-century Spanish friar and mystic St John of the Cross describes his journey into this new world memorably: '*I went into an unknown land unknowing, stayed there knowing naught.*'[2] The journey into stillness is an unknown land that will require from us a spirit of adventure if it is to reveal its gifts to us. But if we can find the courage to make this journey, St John says that we will discover all that we need. Stillness creates space for reflection, and carves out time for pondering the nature of the questions we need to ask. It also seems to me that we can trust the words better that come from our silence. We can have greater faith in the actions that emerge from stillness. They come from somewhere strong and true.

Stillness is not the same as silence. Silence can be an element in the landscape of stillness, and it's vital that we make space for silence, and enjoy it whenever we discover it. But if we imagine that we can only find stillness in silence we will be sorely disappointed. Most of the time the world around us is pretty loud! And there's not a lot that we can do about that. So we need to discover ways to be still *within* a noisy, fast-moving world.

---

2 'After an ecstasy' in *Centred on Love: The Poems of St John of the Cross*, trans. Marjorie Flower OCD, Varrowville: The Carmelite Nuns, 1983.

Slow into Stillness: A Practice

 Stillness needs practice. It's a discipline that needs to be explored, learned and befriended. Almost all the great spiritual traditions have made similar discoveries about the path into stillness. *Slow into Stillness* is my own practice in four steps[3] based on those traditions and my own experience of seeking stillness:

1. Find a space where you can be without distraction. This could be a physical space 'on the ground' marked out perhaps with a cushion, stool or mat, and a candle or icon. It might be a notional space that you create with you when you go for your daily run or walk, or your journey to work.
2. Find a posture that is alert and comfortable. If you are sitting, a reasonably straight back seems to help. Find a way to allow your hands to be at rest, perhaps open with palms up on your lap. You may like to close your eyes.
3. Give attention to your breathing. Most of the time we breathe in a shallow way. That's fine – it's how the body 'ticks over' most of the time. But it's very good for us to learn how to breathe more deeply and slowly from the diaphragm. So breathe deep and slow, giving attention to your breathing. Each breath is a sacred gift. Give space for a brief pause at the end of each breath in and out. The pause matters, carrying with it a quiet sense of momentum and possibility.
4. Now let what I call a *stilling word* or *prayer word* form silently within you. Let the word form in silence in time with your breathing, with each inhalation, with each exhalation. Whenever you become distracted, simply accept this is a fact and return to your word. The stilling word can act as a focus for

---

3 It can be helpful to prepare for this practice by finding a way to express whatever you are feeling, perhaps saying the words that need to be said, thus clearing the way for stillness. A fifth step follows in Practice 9, 'Find Your Stillpoint'.

your thoughts, or as a shield from all the feelings that crash their way in. I have also found how powerful it can be as a statement of my intention. For example, I may use the phrase 'here I am'. As well as being a focus for some thoughts and a shield from others, the prayer word now becomes a statement of my intention to be open and present in stillness to the possibility of the divine, to the mystery, to God. It also acts as a reminder in the Jesus tradition that the Christ has promised 'to be with us always, to the end of the age'.[4] The 'here I am' is both my intention, and his promise.

Enter slow into the unknown land of stillness unknowing – and see what may come into view in this new landscape of possibility.

---

4 Matthew 28.20.

9

Find Your Stillpoint

DRAW A CIRCLE

One late afternoon in early summer
lying on my back in a sunlit room
warm hum of garden-life through the open door,
I draw a circle, and from the floor
watch my hand trace through the air a path
shimmering with signs of the greater life
from which I have come
in which I am held
and to which I will return.
I draw a circle
and am encircled.

The kingdom of God is not coming with things that can be observed; nor will they say, 'Look, here it is!' or 'There it is!' For, in fact, the kingdom of God is among you.

A teaching of Jesus: Luke 17.20b–21

Locating the Stillpoint

Where do you go when everything is in chaos? When life is in turmoil? When everything is in flux? The practice of *Slow into Stillness*[1] marks the beginning of a journey we need to make to

---

1 See Practice 8, 'Slow into Stillness'.

help us face the tough times. The practice of *Find Your Stillpoint* suggests that there is a destination for the stillness path, a place within us to which the journey into stillness is leading. This destination is the stillpoint, the place of beloved belonging, from which a life of stillness and action can flourish, whatever is coming our way. This is the heart of the unknown land on the map of existence marked by St John of the Cross. And it is of course *a state of being* rather than a physical place.

The stillpoint is a place of which we may have been unaware. Perhaps it was previously only glimpsed, or maybe we could not even imagine it. But the contemplative traditions all suggest that this unknown land has always been there waiting for us, within each of us. There is no need to desperately seek something that we don't already have. The gift of stillpoint has been given. You already have it. It is yours and mine. We just need to go to it. And it is *only from this place* that we may face the chaos that sooner or later always comes our way, ride out the storms that sweep in, and run over the rocks that stand in our path.

Dancing at the Stillpoint

The stillpoint has a dynamic quality. Like water in a garden pool, the surface rippling in the breeze, the depths of the pool strong and still. Or perhaps like a slow dance, in which graceful moves emerge from the dancers' still core. Andrei Rublev's much-loved icon-meditation on the life of the Holy Trinity of God reflects this possibility. The three sacred figures are at the same time both absolutely still, and in dynamic relationship. So the stillpoint is not in opposition to movement but enables it and opens it up. In his captivating poem 'Burnt Norton' in *Four Quartets*, T. S. Eliot suggests a fluid, mysterious link between the stillpoint and movement.

At the still point of the turning world. Neither flesh nor
fleshless;

Neither from nor towards; at the still point, there the dance
is . . .[2]

The stillpoint is a dance, and in this dance we will discover our
true nature. In the dance, or in that rippling pool, we will find out,
for example, that we are more than our work, more than what
others think of us, more even than how we see ourselves. That we
are amazing human creatures, streaming with light, flowing with
compassion, and full of goodness. Our stillpoint will also reveal
that we are deeply connected to each other. We are not dancing
alone, and our sense of separation is an illusion. We are connected
to each other, to the planet, to all that exists, to the sacred, to God.
So your suffering is my suffering, my joy is your joy, and everything
that tries to separate us is false. Greater even than connection, a
particular contribution of the Jesus tradition is the discovery at
the stillpoint that we are *loved*. Arrive at the stillpoint and we will
discover Love rising up to meet us.[3]

The Cave of the Heart

The stillpoint is not dependent on our being in any particular
place, sacred or otherwise. This comes out in an interesting story
from the life of Jesus about prayer. The Disciples asked him to teach
them to pray.[4] (This in itself is worthy of note – we can imagine
from this exchange that Jesus' practice of prayer was far less dependent on words than some other teachers of his time, and much
more grounded in contemplative silence than we may have imagined.) In Matthew's setting of this story Jesus teaches the Disciples
to go into their room and shut the door: 'But whenever you pray,

---

2 T. S. Eliot, from 'Burnt Norton' in *Four Quartets, The Complete Poems and Plays of T. S. Eliot*, London: Faber and Faber, 1969.
3 For more on the contribution of the ancient and unfolding Jesus tradition to a contem-
plative life see Practice 46, 'Cave of the Heart (Nurture Your Contemplative)'.
4 Luke 11.1–4.

go into your room and shut the door and pray to your Father who is in secret.'[5]

At first glance this might seem to connect the possibility of still-point to a specific place – your room, behind a closed door. But the monastics have always understood this instruction as being about something other than prayer in a secluded room (although there is of course a long-cherished place in the tradition for that). For them it is a call to discover the 'cave of the heart'. To discover what Jesus describes as the 'kingdom of God' within us. To dwell and to dance in the quiet place at the core of our being. This inner room, this cave of the heart – this stillpoint – is therefore something that we carry with us wherever we go. So wherever you are today, your stillpoint is with you, as close as breathing.

Find Your Stillpoint: A Practice

The practice of *Find Your Stillpoint* is the practice of *Slow into Stillness*[6] continued, ever deeper, ever further. So follow that pattern of still-space, posture, breath and stilling word. Now, if and when you sense you are ready, *let go of the stilling word*, and be attentive to what you may encounter. You are in the stillpoint at the core of your being. In my own experience this may, very occasionally, feel euphoric. Sometimes there may simply be a notion of rest, a hint of joy, a sense that we are not on our own. At other more demanding times, this can feel like absence, darkness, and even loss. This is all very usual. In the Jesus tradition this is described as some kind of experience of God.

The important thing is to stay with the practice. Let it unfold. And give yourself to it. Find your stillpoint, and let your stillpoint find you. As a reminder to engage in your practices of *Slow into Stillness* and *Find Your Stillpoint*, carry or wear a small object that

---

5 Matthew 6.6.
6 See Practice 8, 'Slow into Stillness'.

you associate with stillness, perhaps a stone. Hold or touch the stone, letting its stillness recall you to your stillpoint and draw you into its practice. You have everything that you need to live and flourish this day. At the stillpoint, there the dance is . . .

10

Become Polyphonic

FLYING WITH PALESTRINA

High in the roof of the basilica
some swallows have nested. For
a brief dance in time their undulating lines
and the choir singing Palestrina
become one. A joyful stream
of rolling rhythm and soaring flight
of swooping depth and tenacious spirit
each voice and each wing-beat
singing the oneness of all that meets:
the mixing and the making
the inciting and the imagining
the playing and the praying.
I step out into the street
flying with Palestrina.

(Giovanni Pierluigi da Palestrina was a sixteenth-century Italian composer of
sacred music, and a key figure in the development of the polyphonic style of
choral music.)

*Give therefore to the emperor the things that are the emperor's,
and to God the things that are God's . . .*

A saying of Jesus: Matthew 22.21

Two Talking Heads

Two talking heads. With two opposing views. And only one can be right. Many of our TV and radio news programmes base their content on this simple equation. Get two experts or affected parties on the sofa, and let them battle it out. This may work, but it can encourage a dualistic way of looking at the world, where only one answer is the right answer, and where the last voice speaking wins. In some ways it is much easier to be strongly for or against something. The boundary lines are clear. It's easy to see who's in and who's out, who's right and who's wrong. This kind of dualistic thinking shores up our own sense of rightness. But perhaps something more subtle, more generous and more hopeful is necessary if we are to bring goodness to the world in these demanding times.

This is not to suggest that we let whatever is wrong go unnoticed. We must resist all that dehumanizes us. That will involve making a stand. Nor does it mean that everything that is said, sung or done is equally life-giving or equally true. The issue that needs our attention is that a dualistic way of seeing *some things* can soon become a dualistic way of seeing *everything*. What if life is more about the *both/and* nature of things? What if true maturity involves learning to hold the tensions that occur within and around us? This is both a more nuanced and a more demanding way to live. It may also be a path to freedom.

Finally Comes the Polyphonic

So what might be an alternative? Polyphony (poly = many, phonic = sound or voice) in choral music is created by two or more different but complementary lines being sung at the same time. As the lines interweave, each voice brings something unique and vital to the music. No one voice dominates. Each brings out the best in the others. And through this dance in sound the music can find a fluidity and beauty otherwise unimaginable. If we human beings are to mature, both personally and communally, perhaps we need to see and act in more subtle ways, embracing the paradoxes and holding the contradictions. Finally (we might hope) comes the polyphonic!

This can be a costly process. If we begin to live in a polyphonic way those around us who are more comfortable with a single voice may find our openness to many voices threatening. Jesus himself was on the receiving end of this kind of suspicion. There's a famous story told of Jesus' opponents trying to trap him into giving the wrong answer to a question. It's a legal issue with political, religious and cultural undertones – and carries potentially dangerous implications for Jesus. It's about paying taxes, and whichever way he answers – with a yes or with a no – the Pharisees know he will be trapped.

> Then the Pharisees went and plotted to entrap Jesus in what he said saying, . . . 'Tell us, then, what you think. Is it lawful to pay taxes to the emperor, or not?' But Jesus, aware of their malice, said, 'Why are you putting me to the test, you hypocrites? Show me the coin used for the tax.' And they brought him a denarius. Then he said to them, 'Whose head is this, and whose title?' They answered, 'The emperor's.'[1]

Jesus answers his dualistic critics with a clever and delightful song of polyphony. Give to the emperor what his rightfully his, and to God what is rightfully God's. This polyphonic answer recognizes the different claims being made here, but Jesus is asking a further question of his own, a question about where true worth should be accorded and honour given. What's particularly delightful about Jesus' polyphonic response is that it leaves room for the listener to contribute their own voice. He doesn't spell out what the answer is, but asks us to hear the tune being sung, and work out for ourselves our own response, the line that we'll sing. Those with ears to hear and eyes to see (a favourite playful saying of Jesus) will make the connection. While the tax may go to the emperor, where might true honour go?

---

1 Matthew 22.15–21.

What is Being Unheard?

I call this stance *Become Polyphonic*. It begins, as do so many of these practices, in cultivating a new depth of self-awareness. In this case it's to do with recognizing whenever we are being dualistic, whenever we are excluding, or whenever we are working from a harshly 'right/wrong' principle. When you are next faced with an issue that is causing some disagreement around you, try to step outside of yourself and view your processes of thought and action. Then ask yourself if there might be a bigger picture here that deserves our attention. Can both 'sides' contain some element of truth here? Might there be additional perspectives as yet unheard?

Dualistic thinking is deeply ingrained within us. We can think dualistically about almost anything! Politics and religion might be obvious candidates, but it's just as prevalent in sport, food, music, art and culture. Seeing how far divisive thinking has shaped us can be a sobering experience. But we can and must learn a better way.

Become Polyphonic: A Practice

 A good way into a practice of *Become Polyphonic* is to listen to some polyphonic music – like that of Palestrina. First of all and most importantly, if you like it, simply enjoy the sublime giftedness that this music is to the world! Now take it with you on your mp3 player or just as a musical memory in your head, and the next time you encounter a situation in which there seems to be a strong force urging a single answer that excludes all other points of view, ask yourself if polyphony might have a contribution to make. Then ask yourself, how could you, through your words or actions, begin to create space for a diversity of voices to be heard? How could you *Become Polyphonic*?

11

Be Here, Be Now

RETURNING TO A BLOCK OF STONE

I return
to my tools
and to the bench.
To the morning sunlight slanting in
and to this block of limestone with
our awkward beginnings
so familiar to me now.
Perhaps this will be the day
when the life that is waiting will emerge
when the lover and the beloved will meet.
The stone knows, of course.
It is waiting for me
to give myself completely –
and to sense our becoming.

Jesus asked, 'Who touched me?' When all denied it, Peter said, 'Master, the crowds surround you and press in on you.' But Jesus said, 'Someone touched me; for I noticed that power had gone out from me.'

From the life of Jesus: Luke 8.45–46

Everything You Need

Pause. Take a deep breath in. Then a long breath out. This moment contains everything you need. One of the most freeing outcomes of nurturing a stillness practice is that it helps us discover the present moment. To step into its gift. To immerse ourselves in it. And to be transformed. We have a natural capacity to do this. But this stance of giving ourselves *to the now* needs nurturing. We may sometimes love the present moment, but we seem to have a default setting that swings between what is past and what is future. So we find ourselves lurching from regret for something gone to worry about something yet to come. Or we remember the joy of the past, and hope for the brightness of what may emerge. Those yearnings are fine for what they are, but the present moment is the gift that is given to us. This moment, in all its dulled ordinariness (the common state of things), or in its shining wildness (the occasional state of things), contains all that we need.

Our first attempts to give attention to the present moment can seem awkward and even – if you like to tick off tasks – pointless. It requires a certain humility from us, a recognition that we are not the centre of everything. The present moment puts all our great plans and all our huge disappointments into context. But loving engagement with the present moment is a movement towards freedom. Those plans may still be important, of course, the disappointments still painful. But in giving attention to the present moment we begin to discover another way to see the world, which is equally or even more important. We discover that we don't need to be so fearful or anxious, so proud or ashamed. Those are all attitudes to do with achievement. But attention to the moment hints that there's something more important going on. This moment is connected to all that has gone before, and it will unfold into whatever is to come, but it is of itself the great gift. This is life – and it's here and now!

Who Touched Me?

Jesus seems to have had a deep awareness of the here and now. In the Gospels we find him continually tuned in to the essence of the present moment. The Gospel writer Luke tells a story of Jesus sensing the touch of a nameless woman in a crowd.[1] On his way to a dying girl, and in the midst of the chaos and press of the crowd, Jesus is sufficiently attuned to the moment to notice how one of the many hands reaching out to him comes with a different purpose from the others. Despite the incomprehension of the Disciples he remains focused on what is happening. It's as if all of his life, his calling, even his sense of who he is, is being focused on this moment, and on this woman. Her losses meet his healing, her suffering encounters his compassion. The bigger questions of Jesus' life are finding their meaning for him in the here-and-now of this momentary encounter. Everything else can and must wait for its own moment of presence.

Perhaps a version of his question *Who touched me?* is one that we could take with us as a prayer of intention, or mantra, reminding us of the call to live in the moment. So his *Who touched me?* might become for us: *What is reaching out for my attention?* Or: *Who is engaging with me, unseen or unnoticed?* When we shift our attention to the present moment the people that crowd in on us, and the things that prevent us from getting the job done, may turn out to be where our attention should really focus. Of course the job will probably need doing, but the interruptions of the here-and-now, ironically, may be revealed to be our real work.

Lose Yourself to Find Yourself

The present moment can seem so mundane, but perhaps that's necessary. It's impossible and undesirable to live at a level of permanent high intensity. The here-and-now moments need to feel

1 Luke 8.40–48.

somewhat ordinary in order for us to cope with them. But they can be both ordinary and *good*, ordinary and *mystical*, ordinary and *sacred*. This is what religion at its best seems to show us. It reveals that the ordinary is extraordinary, investing it with dignity and meaning.

So how might we become people of the moment, people who can *Be Here, Be Now*? One way to cultivate a deeper sense of the now is to reflect on the times when we naturally do this. When are you so absorbed in the moment? Any creative act feels most alive when we step into it without noticing time, expectation or distraction. Sex is surely best when we lose ourself fully in the moment. And sport is best when we give ourselves to it. There's almost nothing like that sense of being in the flow of something greater than ourselves. Whenever we lose ourselves, perhaps we find ourselves?

Be Here, Be Now: A Practice

 A good place to begin *Be Here, Be Now* is by giving attention to the things that we do every day as part of our routine, like taking a shower. You can take a shower to become clean, or you can take a shower to take a shower (and also emerge clean!). Notice how the water forms and shapes itself as it flows over you; enjoy the sensation on your skin; wonder at the gift of water and your own connection to it. A next step is to cultivate this stance of attention throughout the day. Be prepared to be surprised.

A deeper step into this practice is to reflect on what might be your least favourite part of your daily routine. Is it, for example, your daily commute to work? Is it possible that what you have tried to ignore, get through or move on from as fast as possible may turn out to be a gift? What might change if you give yourself to this moment? In time perhaps even the packed-train experience might evolve into something more positive, more hopeful, and even sacred.

12

Live Transparent

TRANSPARENT

I have always loved the way
that you have lived transparent, clear
a shining rock-pool, here
without deception or manipulation
without fear or envy or cruel intention.

So may I come to wade in your transparency
and walk my sideways walk, to slowly
run my hand through these grains of sand
to bring my hiddenness into light, and
take my place and catch my breath
and find my own clarity
shone through?

'The eye is the lamp of the body. So, if your eye is healthy, your whole body will be full of light; but if your eye is unhealthy, your whole body will be full of darkness.'

A teaching of Jesus: Matthew 6.22–23a

Clarity of Water

If one fine day I'm blessed enough to have grandchildren, rock-pooling will be just about top of the list of the things I will want to do with them. As well as introduce them to the Kung Fu Panda Po, football in the back garden, St John of the Cross, the ferry to Iona, Jackson Pollock, J. S. Bach and REM. Heh, look at me anticipating a walk on the reckless side of grand-parenting. But equipped with a bucket and net, and a steely determination to see out the first few cold minutes, this small world of rocks, sand and seaweed (weed? – how much of a mis-naming is that for these beautiful plants?) will be ours to explore, full of rippling light and mysterious life. We'll catch some shrimps, dance around skittish shore crabs, and perhaps scoop a few small fish into our nets. And we'll enjoy the clarity of the water that swept in with the last high tide, the true glory of the rock pool, its transparency a thing of wonder.

Live Transparent is a stance of stillness and movement for a life to bring good to us and to the world around us. It's about living with openness. Most of us have probably found ourselves at some time living without transparency. Keeping the water cloudy. And it doesn't feel good. Lives and societies that bring good thrive on openness. Living transparent doesn't mean that we have to put everything 'out there'. There will be private things, precious things, intimate and tough things that need to be held just by us and by the people we love and the people who love us. There's a place for reserve, for reticence, and for the best kind of hiddenness, that born out of humility. But this stance is about setting out to live in a transparent way. Could transparency become our first instinct rather than our last recourse?

Being Seen and Seeing

So where might we start? There are aspects of social media that we need to be careful about, but it seems to me that they can offer a real opportunity to embrace transparency. Wherever and when-ever we choose to create a public profile we have the opportunity to share something of who we are and what shapes us. So I hope that, in whatever context you know me, you'll recognize the *me* that I share on Facebook and Twitter. Of course I don't put all of my life there. But I hope that whatever you see there rings true about me, holds together with integrity and reflects the hopeful human being that I'm trying to become (through my flaws).

If our willingness to *be seen* is vital, the way that we *see* is just as important. Jesus emphasizes the importance of how we decide to see the world. 'If your eye is healthy,' he teaches, 'your whole body will be full of light.' He seems to be saying that if we aspire to *see* with clarity, we will begin to *live* with clarity. On the other hand if we choose to ignore the way things truly are around us, and in the wider world, we'll gradually become less resistant to misinformation, manipulation and untruths. And our own lives will cloud up. So if to *Live Transparent* is to open ourselves up where appropriate to *be seen*, it's also about *coming to see* clearly. To look with clarity (but without hasty judgement) at what is happening around us.

Specks and Planks

The integrity of transparent living has to start with us. It doesn't work well for us to point out the murkiness of a pool that belongs to someone else or to some other institution if our own pool is cloudy and disturbed. Jesus seems to have reserved some of his strongest comments for people who focus on the faults of others – how easily, he says, we see the speck in someone else's eye, while ignoring the plank in our own[1] (Jesus is often in the prophetic tradition of telling a story boldly). Seeing clearly is about looking for the truth around us, but the search for the truth must begin within us.

I hope that by this point you are beginning to sense how this series of practices of stillness and movement hang together. Living transparent, for example, only becomes possible when we come to realize, in stillness, that we are deeply connected, even loved. The

---

1 Matthew 7.1–5.

practice of finding our stillpoint locates us in a place of connection and love, so that we can let the light fall on us without fear. Our regrets and 'failings' are still real, but they are not what defines us. I'll say more about our shadows and darknesses later, but suffice to say here that the light of transparency need not be feared, and can in fact help us to become reconciled to the tougher aspects of our character. Once we begin to choose transparency we are more free to truly become the people we want to be. We will discover that there really is no need to be suspicious, fearful or ashamed. No need to pretend, contrive or manipulate any longer. All that we have been, all that we are, and all that we may one day become will find their belonging.

Live Transparent: A Practice

 A way into the practice of *Live Transparent*: Whenever you make a statement about yourself today, in word or action, online or in person, ask yourself how you might do this with (appropriate) transparency. Will those receiving whatever you are saying or doing recognize something that is truthfully of you in this?

I wonder what might change if even a small number of us committed ourselves to attempting to *Live Transparent*? How far might the ripples spread out? Could we grow a culture of transparency wherever we are – at home, at work, in our communities? This may be a costly step. Inevitably some people will feel threatened and undermined by the transparency of others. But if it is embraced with strength and humility, its work and effect will be real and lasting. And so may you encounter the amazing freedom of your *own clarity, shone through.*

13

Love Your Roots

THE MEMORY OF SONGS

Slowly, gratefully an epiphany
the presence of something extraordinary:
a quiet tumbling of cascading notes,
shining chords and
calling bells

My attention shifting from the task in my hands
to the mystery of sounds, the memory of songs
an ancient echo. I put down my pen
and go to the radio in the kitchen.

So this is how the sacred gift is passed on!
A subtle movement perceived at the edge
of vision, grasses swaying in the breeze:
a quiet tumbling of cascading notes,
shining chords and
calling bells

The sound of the cosmos, of life, of love:
Arvo Pärt's 'Cantus in Memoriam Benjamin Britten'.

(Arvo Pärt (b. 1935) is an Estonian composer of classical and sacred music.)

Now Philip was from Bethsaida, the city of Andrew and Peter. Philip found Nathanael and said to him, 'We have found him about whom Moses in the law and also the prophets wrote, Jesus son of Joseph from Nazareth.' Nathanael said to him, 'Can anything good come out of Nazareth?'

From the life of Jesus: John 1.44–46

We Need Roots

It's complicated. For thousands of years people with origins all over the world have found their home in the islands we call Britain. I am one such. I know almost nothing of my father except his surname which may be either English or Irish. On my birth-mother's side I had a Jewish refugee grandmother who fled Nazi-dominated Germany as a young woman just before the Second World War. My grandfather may have come from France. I was adopted as a baby by an English-British couple. So the story is complicated. Some of it is painful. Much of the story is missing. But it's the story into which I've been born and which I have accepted as my own. I've slowly come to realize how important it is that I love (wherever) I've come from.

'*We need roots*,'[1] sing the English folk duo Show of Hands, expressing a common sense of loss that many experience in a globally-connected-but-disconnected world. The song continues:

And we learn to be ashamed before we walk
of the way we look and the way we talk
Without our stories or our songs
how will we know where we've come from?

Knowing where we come from and accessing the best qualities of that tradition can bring a quiet sense of belonging, purpose

---

1 'Roots' by Show of Hands on the album *Witness*.

and direction. Wherever we are in the world, we stand in a line of people whose wisdom, hope and yearning has been shaped by their setting. Whatever people, tribe, nationality or religion, it's good to know where we've come from, to mourn the problematic episodes and celebrate the good things in our heritage. We need to enter our collective memory. And to love our roots!

Identity as a Gift

There are some tensions here. If we imagine our roots as circles of belonging we need to deal with the reality that others are of course beyond the edges of our circle, and in different circles. These tensions can be negotiated but we need to be aware of them. Tribalism and nationalism need particular care. At their best they can represent dynamic links to our settings and stories. At their worst they can encourage an exclusive, inward focus that means our story is exclusive and excluding. This raises important questions. How, for example, can we celebrate our national identity without denigrating others or identifying ourselves as against others? How does nationalism work for people with a complicated or multi-stranded sense of identity (like me)? And if nationalism could truly mature, might it actually drop away, allowing us to focus on the greater task of being human beings, bringing good to each other and to the world?

It's vital to ask how our national identity can be a gift to people of other national identities (and vice versa). I wonder if it's at all possible for nationalism to help us into the essential task of deepening our sense of being part of common wider humanity? I think it is, but it's a fine line that needs approaching with care. Here's an excerpt from another beautiful song in the folk tradition that I think manages to do that, suggesting how local life and culture might be a potential gift to the wider world. It's Maggie Holland's 'A Place Called England':

And come all you at home with freedom
Whatever the land that gave you birth
There's room for you both root and branch
As long as you love the English earth[2]

Love God and Love Neighbour

The Palestine that Jesus knew was familiar with national tensions. The provinces of Galilee and Judea were conquered territories of the dominant Roman empire, and many of their people dreamed of and worked for the overthrow of the foreign invader. It would have been understandable for Jesus to have shared this view. His entire life of teaching and healing took place in a relatively small area, and he seems to have been happy to have been identified with his hometown in the north of Israel, Nazareth, even though that part of the country may have been seen as an uncultured backwater – witness the disciple Nathanael's curt 'Can anything good come out of Nazareth?'[3] One of the arguments used by the religious authorities against Jesus in their attempts to get the local Roman governor to execute him was that he was an agitator against the empire. But in fact we don't find a nationalist Jesus in the Gospels. Rather, we find a healer and teacher who is calling the people of Galilee and Judea to love God and to love neighbour. To draw on their old story as Israel-Judah, a people seeking to become a sign of God's goodness in the world. This is the greater task.

---

2 'A Place Called England' by Maggie Holland.
3 John 1.46.

Love Your Roots: A Practice

 Within the bigger picture of becoming goodness – of becoming truly human – the practice of *Love Your Roots* is about nurturing awareness of the streams that have shaped you and your people. It's about cultivating a sense of the giftedness in those roots and looking for ways to allow those gifts to be shared. It's also about deciding to reject or reshape whatever may be the opposite of gift, the difficult aspects of your tradition that damage and dehumanize. And it's about respecting people of other roots and engaging with them in a spirit of honour and friendship. For some this may be relatively easy. You may come from a place with a strong and generous sense of self-worth, history and beauty. But if you come from somewhere with a more complicated sense of its own evolution this may be a tougher task. But please be encouraged. Can anything good come from your story, from your setting, from your place, from your town? Of course it can, and it already is, in you and in others like you.

The stance of *Love Your Roots* begins with reflection. Where are your roots? How has the identity of your people (or peoples – if like me you can identify various strands of belonging) been formed? How have those roots shaped your own story? Now look for ways to step with humility and strength into the best of your tradition, and pray for grace to hold in tension the difficult things in that tradition that can no longer be changed. A sign of maturity in this area may be our ability to honour the roots of others as much as we love our own roots.

14

Into the Music

ELEVEN HUNDRED MILES NORTH WEST

Eleven hundred miles north west the Boy Lilikoi
sifted stones for sounds, and blessed
with a gold-panner's intuition sieved
the earth elements of a song that lives
and always lived, waiting to be discovered
then sung across the Northern seas, a lover
opening love's irresistible possibility:
you too can burn so bright!

('Boy Lilikoi' is a song by the Icelandic musician Jonsi.)

When (Jesus) came to Nazareth, where he had been brought up,
he went to the synagogue on the sabbath day, as was his custom.
He stood up to read, and the scroll of the prophet Isaiah was given
to him. He unrolled the scroll and found the place where it was
written:

'The Spirit of the Lord is upon me,
because he has anointed me
to bring good news to the poor.
He has sent me to proclaim release to the captives
and recovery of sight to the blind,
to let the oppressed go free,
to proclaim the year of the Lord's favour.'

From the life of Jesus: Luke 4.16–19

Metal Guru is it You?

Sometimes I find myself inside a blissful dream, in which I've been handed a trumpet. I know I can't play it but I put my lips to the mouthpiece and ever so tentatively blow. To my surprise (I know I can't play it) and unlike other musical dreams (like being on stage, behind a drum kit, the band expecting me to begin but I can't make a beat) the sound that emerges is good. I raise the trumpet to my lips again, and a beautiful sound forms. I play on, tears streaming down my face.

Today as I wake an idea forms for the day ahead. Today I will try to live again like 'So What'.[1] Through all the stuff, in the challenging tasks and in the welcome happenings, I will aspire to live today like this piece of music by Miles Davis. Relaxed, with momentum and possibility, free to take the tune – and life – in new directions. I know that there will be things today that will disrupt this idea, but it's a very good place to start.

I sense the truth in the suggestion that '*All art constantly aspires towards the condition of music*'.[2] Great music has the ability to both tell a story and create space for a new story to emerge. It's not a competition among the arts, of course, and all art does this, but perhaps music has a unique ability to work within us, reaching into our head and heart, hands and feet.

There's a theory that the way most of us access music now – downloading an electronic file from a huge omni-present online resource – means that people's relationship with music is changing. That may be true, but I sense that our love for music and its capacity to shape us and to shape our world will always carry the day. The way that we access the music will continue to change, but the music will always do its brilliant work in, on and through us. In the summer of 1972 T Rex's 'Metal Guru' jumped out at me from a tinny transistor radio. And something changed for me in

---

1 The opening track to Miles Davis's *Kind of Blue* album.
2 Walter Pater, 1839–94.

that moment. The world looked totally different. *Metal Guru is it you? (Oh yeah!)*

Music as Sacrament

I'm interested in the way music has a capacity to bring something new, unknown or forgotten into being. This is a mysterious and wonderful thing. Sometimes a piece of music comes our way that seems to know something about us that we perhaps suspected but didn't know, or felt but couldn't name. Theologians have a name for this process. They call it sacramental, and it seems to me that music can be a sacrament. A sacrament both signposts what is true, and opens up space for, or even brings into being, the reality that it points to. When music acts in this way it discloses something about what it is like to be human, and in its making and hearing it enables the maker and the hearer to enter more deeply into that experience.

So the adventurous spirit of Miles Davis's 'So What' points to the adventurous spirit that is already present in me. As I respond to that insight today, the adventurous spirit in me will be re-ignited and given new life. In this way music can help us find our true selves, and to live out of that rediscovery. The music can uncover a stream of life hidden deep under our surface, a river of vitality that we may barely recognize. But whenever it appears we'll realize that it was there all the time.

When Jesus Played Jazz

There's something very special about making music. Music always has the capacity to take us into something much greater than ourselves. Playing, making and singing music has a particular capacity to do this. Something mysterious can happen when a group of players begin to make music. Some kind of intuitive spirit can take over, in which the individuals become less conscious of their own playing, and the communal nature of the music comes to the fore. We find that the music has a life of its own. The music transcends its playing and its players. The song was always there. We are just tapping into it. Or maybe it is finding us?!

Jesus played jazz. Luke sets the beginning of the public life of Jesus in a dramatic scene.[3] Jesus has come to his hometown of Nazareth. He has come back to his local roots. And he has come to the synagogue, his religious home. Asked to read a passage from the Jewish scriptures, he reads from the prophet Isaiah. In a few sentences Jesus sets himself firmly within the context of his people's old story, their learning and their yearnings. Jesus is entering into a song that has been played and sung for centuries. But there is also an unmistakable sign that he is going to do something new with this song that springs from the tradition, something that will be a gift to a much wider audience than just his own people. It's a supreme moment of religious and cultural jazz, loving the tradition, sensing a new line coming into being.

Into the Music: A Practice

The practice of *Into the Music* is about entering the wonder, the wisdom and the wildness of music. At one level it's simply about engaging with the music that we love (or may learn to love). 'Bathe yourself in the healing power of music,' writes my partner in the StillPoint project, Matt Rees.[4] But beyond this it's about entering the deeper life-music into which this heard-or-played music is taking us. 'Allow it to name and give voice to your inner world,' Matt goes on to say.

Like many of the practices in *Running Over Rocks* this begins with nurturing awareness. This is not about being analytical, but simply recognizing how music works in and on you. Be curious

---

3 Luke 4.16–20.
4 Matt Rees: www.home-online.org/2012/05/into-the-music-matts-talk.

about the music that moves you. What is going on here? And if you have ever had the idea of learning an instrument, or starting to sing, or picking up again what you once tried, may today be the day when you begin to do something about it.

Then ask yourself what the deeper life-song might be that the music is calling you into. One of the most joyous earthy-spiritual experiences that I've had recently was at a gig by Jonsi.[5] It was my experience of hearing one of his songs – 'Boy Lilikoi' – that inspired the poem 'Eleven hundred miles north west'. At one level I just love the music, but at another his adventures in image and sound seem to work in me in a much deeper way, inspiring me to continue my attempts to walk the path as a human being trying to bring goodness to the world. To keep on moving *Into the Music*.

---

5 www.jonsi.com; www.sigur-ros.co.uk.

PRACTICES OF DESCENT

From anxiety towards acceptance:
navigating the tough times

This artwork began as a quickly painted study of a diving figure, and became a slow meditation on entering Lent.

We all know what it's like to fall. After all, we've been doing it since we were small children. And of course experiences of falling don't stop when we learn to walk and run. Things go wrong. Bad things happen. Tragedies come our way. We find ourselves in low places. This is part of what it means to be human. And there seems to be a sense that they are a natural part of existence. That we can't have the wonder without the desolation.

This series of practices helps us to negotiate the tough times whenever they come, as come they surely will. Descent is one of the realities of existence. But it contains within its harshness the possibility for our flourishing. This is not just about surviving the tough times but about learning to stay with them, to receive their learning, and to find the means to be ready for an ascent when that becomes possible. This is about leaning into the gaps, giving space to the sharp declines, falling to the dark ground and somehow finding there the resources we will need once more to run over rocks.

The seasons connected with these Practices of Descent are Lent, Passiontide and Holy Week. In these seasons the tradition enters the darkness, failure and abandonment experienced by Jesus. His own story of descent becomes a pattern through which we may learn to face our own descents. The Christ's experience is ours, and ours is his.

15

Let Go (Keep on Letting Go)

SEA-SWIMMING

Sea-swimming and I
feared I was drowning.
Into deep is in too deep.
I can see myself so small on the surface
then slowly
spiralling
down
falling
failing flailing
wrapped in darkness.

But this is prayer
and this is life
and you are held
so let go and breathe
into deep.

Going a little farther, (Jesus) threw himself on the ground and prayed that, if it were possible, the hour might pass from him.

From the life of Jesus: Mark 14.35

The Sinking of the *Mary Rose*

A shiver. The fear of deep water. As a child of seven or eight I remember being frightened but captivated by an image in a magazine. It was of a painting of the sinking in the Solent in July 1545 of Henry VIII's great flagship, the *Mary Rose*. Frightened sailors plunge into the sea as the great ship keels over so fast that the majority on board will be drowned within a couple of minutes. Around the same time as I saw this I was rolled by a big wave on a beach at Morar on the west coast of Scotland. So sea-swimming is always a challenge! But I love it too. Swimming out beyond my own depth, facing the sun, held by the water, at one with the sea, can be a beautiful and even sacred experience. In this moment nothing else matters. But it requires me to let go, and to keep on letting go, and it has helped shape this practice.

Let Go (Keep on Letting Go) is about nurturing a sense that the first step towards changing something difficult is to accept that it is real. And then realizing that however bad it is, it does not have to destroy us. Letting go will almost certainly feel counter-intuitive. But there's something immensely strong in discovering that we can not only face the descent but remain with it. And we need to learn this skill. Everything in our being may be urging us to flee, but if we learn how to stay with it, to look the falling in the eye, it will begin to lose its power over us. And we may even discover that in this experience of descent there could be some dark gift that will help us one day to make an ascent, however remote that possibility may appear now.

The Falling

There are no easy short-cuts to letting go. This is a courageous practice that demands much of us. In the Jesus tradition there are resources that can help us to embrace this stance. However fast our fall, however disorienting and however consuming it feels to

us, the tradition suggests that the real centre of gravity lies else-
where. Jesus was no stranger to the experience of descent. On the
night before his crucifixion we encounter him in the Garden of
Gethsemane. He has a cold insight into what may happen to him,
and is, says Mark, deeply disturbed. He prays that he may be ex-
cused the cup of suffering that seems to be coming his way. He is in
descent – and he is very real about how that feels. But he comes to
a point where he finds words of letting go: 'Abba, Father, for you all
things are possible; remove this cup from me; yet, not what I want,
but what you want.'[1]

This letting go by Jesus is not a rolling over in the face of defeat,
nor is it the last resigned act of someone with nowhere else to go.
It is rather an acceptance by Jesus that there may be something
bigger and deeper going on, that the descent may somehow be
trusted. At this stage there is no sign of ascent. His letting go is
complete. So the Jesus path suggests that the descent is not just
navigable, but in some ways essential. The falling is important. It
teaches us what we need to learn to live.

The Buoyancy of Water

How can we nurture this stance of letting go? Again this begins in
self-awareness. If you are able to, go for a swim, and try to remember what courage it may have taken you the very first time you
learned to float unaided. Everything seems to tell us that swimming shouldn't work! At first we feel clumsy and vulnerable in the
water, both heavy and minuscule. But as you swim, see how you
feel in the water now. When we trust ourselves to it, when we let
go of the pool-side and of the life-aid, we discover the amazing
buoyancy of water. See how this letting go has freed you to swim!

If I have a big event coming up there's perhaps a one in five
chance that on the morning of the event I will wake up with what

---

1 Mark 14.36.

feels like a knot in my stomach. It's not pleasant, I wish it wouldn't happen, but it happens and there it is. I've gradually discovered that it's much better to let go of my desire that the knot wasn't there. To accept it. Even to learn to welcome it as a friend. And to offer care and attention to the knot. Somehow it then seems to work *with* me rather than *against* me, and when the event happens I may end up offering something helpful, rather than being focused on my own experience of descent.

Let Go (Keep on Letting Go): A Practice

 Here's a way into the practice of *Let Go (Keep on Letting Go)*. The next time you have a descent experience, in your imagination try to step outside of yourself and notice how you react to it. Pay close attention to how it makes you feel physically. What does this descent feel like in your body? How does it show itself? Then see how it might work not to suppress this, but to allow the physical feeling to happen, trusting that you will be held. Like the causes of the descent, its symptoms may not be pleasant. But it may be possible, with courage and practice, to learn to accept, and even to befriend, those sensations. This is *not* about welcoming whatever has caused the descent. But it is about letting go of our resistance to the *physical feelings* the descent seems to create in us. It can be helpful to have a prayer or mantra to accompany this letting go. Here's one I've created:

' *, I welcome you.
May you be blessed.
May your energy unfurl within me
And so may I bring blessing today.'

* the name of the uncomfortable physical feeling of descent

It makes no rational sense to let go of everything that gives us security. But when we begin to trust ourselves to the spaciousness that opens up, to *Let Go* and *Keep on Letting Go*, something interesting happens. But first we have to be ready to remain wherever the descent takes us, to sit with the darkness.

16

Sit with the Darkness

BUT THE DARKNESS (AFTER THE PROLOGUE)

The light shone in the darkness
but the darkness has overcome it
vast and overwhelming, complete.

The word once uttered is silent
confined to memory's fragile
fragments, scattered.

The body that warmed is
slab-cold and indifferent,
turned away, gone.

The bell that rang its rhythm and rumour
hangs still in the morning
witness to nothing, dumb.

The angels that came unseen
have been usurped, the
wild beasts surround me.

The light shone in the darkness
but the darkness has overcome it.

Blessed are those who mourn, for they will be comforted.

A teaching of Jesus: Matthew 5.4

When the Light Goes Out

Autumn was sliding into winter, the south-west peninsula stuck in an angry stream of Atlantic gales. And I was going through an unusually dark season. Usually I am a very hopeful person. But at this time it felt as if whatever hope there was had long abandoned me. I tried to write my way out of it, but the growing darkness was sapping my energy. One dark afternoon I found some words coming into being within me which became the core of the poem 'But the darkness (after the prologue)'.

It felt as if the light had been extinguished. This is a tough situation for anyone. For one who aspires to be a follower of the one who described both himself[1] and his followers[2] as the Light of the World, it comes with a whole new set of demanding questions. John's Gospel has a reflective and poetic character, and the imaginative and profound prologue to the Gospel pivots on the idea that however dark everything seems to become, the light cannot be extinguished. But that's how it felt to me that autumn-becoming-winter.

Here's the interesting thing. A kind of turning point came once I accepted that there really was no light, and as I then wrote that sense of complete darkness into the poem. Once I found the courage to accept that the light had been extinguished, something somewhere began to change. After a while I began to sense a tiny pin-prick of light, some fragile flickering, out of sight. Everything didn't change then, of course. But ever so gradually, like the dawning of one of those autumn storm-days, the darkness began to lift.

Holy Saturday

One of the dark gifts in the tradition that has emerged around the Jesus story is the event we call Holy Saturday, a remembering of the

---

1 John 8.12.
2 Matthew 5.14.

often neglected centre of the story of the death and resurrection of Jesus. Neglected, I think, because it is so dark. As the day of Jesus' execution draws to a close a few friends – Joseph of Arimathea, Mary Magdalene, 'the other Mary'[3] and Nicodemus – obtain permission to take his body down from the cross. They prepare the body for burial with spices and linen wrappings, and lay it in a garden tomb.[4] The tomb is sealed with a large stone. And that's it. The one who spoke of light is now in darkness. The one who healed bodies is a body torn apart. The one who claimed to bring life is dead. The mourners are left to mourn. Some bewildered followers prepare to return to their homes in the hills around Jerusalem. Others shut themselves away for fear that they too will be caught up in the retribution for Jesus' perceived challenge to the system.

The tradition remembers this dark story by *entering it*. As Good Friday closes, in tiny churches and in huge cathedrals, in simple chapels and in ornate sanctuaries, wherever the event is remembered, the building is left to fall into darkness. Candles are extinguished. Altars are stripped. Icons and statues are covered in dark cloths. The doors are closed and the people leave. This is Holy Saturday. And the vital thing is that this is done without anticipation of change. We enter the darkness as if there will never be light. We choose to forget the Easter Vigil that will follow, with its gradual lighting of candles, its baptism of new believers, and ultimately its joyous acclamations of rising. To truly enter the spirit of Holy Saturday this must all be laid aside. We must lie down in the tomb, as the theologian Michelle Trebilcock memorably says, dead with the dead God.[5] There is no hope. All is lost.[6]

---

3 Matthew 27.57–61.

4 John 19.41.

5 Michelle Trebilcock, 'Living with Jesus in Liminality: An invitation to be dead with the dead God', *Crucible* 4:1, April 2012, www.reddresstheology.com/writing.

6 See the artwork 'All is lost' by Ian Adams: www.ianadams.info.

Sitting Shivah

One of the foundational sayings of Jesus is his call to be alongside others in their experience of darkness. *Blessed are those who mourn*, he says, *for they shall be comforted.* To mourn with those who suffer is a blessed thing, blessed for both the ones suffering and for those who come alongside them. As a rabbi Jesus would have been very familiar with the sort of mourning practices that have evolved and been shaped into the contemporary Jewish practice of Sitting Shivah (the Hebrew word for seven).

This is the practice of mourning for a close relative for seven days following the burial of the body. The bereaved sit in their home in silence. No work is attempted. No greetings are exchanged. Mourners sit low to the ground on stools, cushions or low benches, a reminder of the earthy nature of human life and the resting place for the human body in death. If the bereaved wish to speak of their loved one, then their visitors may respond. An item of clothing may be torn at the funeral, then worn throughout the period of Shivah, a sign of the tearing nature of grief, and possibly a link directly back into ancient Jewish practice of wearing sackcloth and ashes. In Sitting Shivah space is being created to enable the feelings of loss and grief to be fully experienced. All attention is given to the work of grief. The dead are honoured. Those left behind are being enabled to engage fully in their loss.

Sit with the Darkness: A Practice

 The practice of *Sit with the Darkness* is about giving ourselves to the darknesses that come our way. Making a decision to live with them, to live in them, to live out from them. This is how healing, hope and light may eventually find their way back to us. There is no short-cut to light. And there is no easy way to discover the wisdom of sitting with darkness. We have to enter it, we have to experience it for ourselves. But we can prepare ourselves for it. And we can be with others who are experiencing darkness.

Begin by allowing your own losses, griefs and darknesses to find a space. They and you have to be given room to find each other. Find your own way to do this, perhaps in an act of creativity or in a conversation. Allow the feelings, images or actions to take shape in a way that is not damaging to the people around you, but very real about what you are feeling. The practice then takes on a new and generous quality by finding ways to be with the people around you in their darknesses. Look for the right time to be a quiet presence with someone in their suffering.

The practice of Sitting Shivah is wary of words. Becoming at ease when words fail is another key practice for negotiating the descents and falls that come our way.

17

Speak No Words

FLYING A KITE (IN A HURRICANE)

Gasping for breath that will not come
I'm flying a kite in a hurricane
  the strings tearing into my
    hands tethered to a
      snapping speck
      of red in an
        angry
        sky
        ...
        ..
        .

         .

          .

           .

            .

             .

              .

               .

Pilate asked (Jesus) again, 'Have you no answer? See how many charges they bring against you.' But Jesus made no further reply, so that Pilate was amazed.

From the life of Jesus: Mark 15.4–5

Face Down on the Ground

I'm aware of the irony of writing any words at all for a practice entitled *Speak No Words*. So I'm just offering a few, then leaving space for silence. Sometimes it is fine to run out of words. Helpful, important, even necessary. As Jesus demonstrated in his own use of silence before his accusers, there can be learning and healing through abandoning our words which, important as they can be, try to do so much fixing, so much arranging and so much explaining. Sometimes the very best thing, sometimes the *only* thing, is to lie face down on the ground, and say nothing.

Speak No Words: A Practice

no words

18

Come to the Edge

WALK WITH ME

Walk with me to the bay
to where the cliff falls away
to the sea
and sit with me
where the kestrel hovers on the rising breeze
where the thrift clings tender in tenacity
where the swallow swoops and dips, brave
where the light catches each rising wave
where the rock splinters from its ancient wall
where the beach gathers its plastic haul.

Walk with me to the bay
to where the cliff falls away
to the sea
and sit with me.

Foxes have holes, and birds of the air have nests; but the Son of Man has nowhere to lay his head.

A teaching of Jesus: Matthew 8.20

The Land is Shifting

The edges are moving. The land is shifting. Each time I walk on the South West Coast Path I can see that there are subtle changes to the meeting point of land and sea. This edge between the landscape and seascape is constantly evolving as storm and wind, sand and stone, tide and current engage with each other. A path that we could take just three years ago on the sand dunes has now disappeared. The debris from ancient tides is being exposed. This week the beach has a huge new swathe of pebbles and drying black seaweed dumped by a storm-driven high tide.

I'm very interested in the idea of what I'll call *edge space* as being the place where change for good can happen. Edge space is threshold or liminal space, and offers a way into something new. It's the site of potential transition, transformation, and deep change. Edge space can be encountered in a physical place, like the cliff in the poem 'Walk with me', but it's a much wider idea than geography. Every task that feels beyond you is edge space. Every decision about your life direction is an edge space. Every new day is an edge space!

Boundaries bring safety. So if you like closure, clear beginnings and neat endings, edge space will be particularly demanding. It's the place beyond safe space. We cannot predict or guarantee the outcome. So it can be an uncomfortable place, even seemingly dangerous. But it is the place of great possibility. The beachboulder field that I ran over as a child was an edge space. I didn't know what it would do to me. I didn't know if I would emerge unscathed. To bring good to the world we have to give ourselves to this place of possibility.

Dance of the Pulsating Present

Jesus seems to have practised walking the edge. His wandering lifestyle is one continuous walk through edge space, where he is open to encounter the unexpected event, and reliant on the welcome of strangers and friends. Unlike the foxes and birds, 'the Son of Man', he says (speaking of himself), 'has nowhere to lay his head'. In Luke's version of this story, we find Jesus making this statement as he 'sets his face' towards Jerusalem, despite the fact (or because?) he knows that this is potentially a dangerous place. He is moving in a direction that may bring to fulfilment what he senses is his calling. But it is also likely to be a journey into suffering. Perhaps he realizes that in his case the two are inextricably linked. But he senses that the edge path is the only route to take if he is to be true to his spirit.

The possibility of edge space runs through all the practices that I suggest are at the root of the Jesus tradition (see Practices 43–48). Contrary, for example, to how we might imagine it, the Eucharist (the Mass, the Communion, the Lord's Supper) is a supreme (even the supreme) edge space. How could it be anything else! The locus of heaven and earth touching. The ancient past, the pulsating present and the unimagined future dancing together. The focused presence of the community that is God and the saints. Perhaps that's why the Eucharist is usually experienced as a humble thing. If we could see this particular edge space for what it truly is we might not be able to handle its awesome reality. For two millennia those practising the Jesus tradition have found it to be truly a transformative place.

Into the Wide Open

It's important to see the edge as wide open space rather than as a narrow path. That's a deception for which we can often fall – that there's only one good possible outcome, an outcome that may be denied to us or that we may miss. No, the edge is an open space full of possibility. Walking the edge is not an ever-shrinking and narrowing path but a journey into an ever-widening space for possibility for good.

Jesus' practice of the edge meant that he was able to face his ultimate challenges. He still experienced fear, he still felt grief, he still suffered. But he was able to live those challenges with calmness and clarity. To see them through. And, in the end, to absorb all the world's uncertainties, all our painful open-endedness, all our edge spaces; to hold them; and to transform them. The tradition recognizes the experience of Jesus on the cross as the ultimate edge space. And his willingness to remain there as a gift to all people, indeed to the whole cosmos. Although we may not recognize it, in this act all of our edge spaces have been held and transformed.

Come to the Edge: A Practice

 I'm calling this practice *Come to the Edge*. Begin to allow the open-ended nature of any *situation* you face to become a source of possibility rather than a source of anxiety. This will almost certainly feel unnatural at first. It's another practice that needs practice! But as we do this we may discover that we have a capacity for it. The edge will begin to feel like a natural home for us.

The idea of welcoming notional edge spaces can be nurtured in a physical way. I'm not advocating that you take up a dangerous sport (although, with the right training, equipment and advice you might choose to explore something adventurous). But I am suggesting that you make it a regular practice to do something that engages you in edge space. This should be something that links to your sense of calling.[1] So perhaps take a walk along the edge of a river, lake or sea. Start a new piece of work. Talk to a stranger. Do the something which you know makes you fearful, but which you also sense may open up the next stage of your own being and doing. Come to the edge *where the cliff falls away to the sea*.

---

1 See Practice 24, 'Find your Deep Flow'.

19

Befriend Your Shadow

MORNING WORDS

I wake, and reach out but
your side of the bed is undisturbed
and there is no warm folding into
each other. Your absence
coils itself around me, the
cold outline of your memory
beginning to fade in detail and
sharpen in loss. I whisper
our morning words, but
you are not here.

*In gathering the weeds you would uproot the wheat along with
them. Let both of them grow together until the harvest.*

A parable of Jesus: Matthew 13.29–30a

Hiding a Shadow in the Shadows

Time to enter the shadowlands. Here, astonishingly, we may discover that the aspects of our being that we've felt to be sources of weakness, failure or shame may contain the possibility for our flourishing. We may have thought that we needed to pretend that these 'flaws' didn't exist. We may have tried to overcome them, to push them down, or even to destroy them. In Jungian psychology this area of our character is called the shadow. Whenever we resist or suppress our shadow, whenever we try to hide our shadow in the shadows, it just seems to pop up somewhere else, and may actually increase in capacity for destruction. It's sobering to realize how easily we recognize and condemn the same traits in others as a way of suppressing the shadow within ourselves. The reality is that we need to come to know our shadows, to accept where they have come from and, crucially, to trust that they carry within them the seeds of their own transformation. We need to give them care and attention. We may even need to give them our love.

I'm calling this practice *Befriend Your Shadow*. As with so many of the *Running Over Rocks* life practices, this one requires us to nurture our self-awareness. It needs us to take a clear view of our instincts and patterns, our motivations and behaviours, our desires and our actions. This needs to be done, initially at least, without judgement. My own experience of this work is that my shadow is intimately linked to my light. It's not a foreign body that has attached itself to me or wormed its way into me. Rather, my shadow is my joy off-balance, my hope submerged, my love trampled. And I couldn't have the light without the shadow.

Wheat and Weeds Together

So what do we do with our shadow once we begin to notice it? Jesus tells a parable of what he calls the kingdom. This, he says, is what the life of God is like, and how life among us could be. The parable is a farming story. A host of weeds have taken hold in a field of wheat, introduced by an enemy of the farmer. There's a debate about whether to uproot the weeds. The farmer decides that to do this would also uproot the wheat. So the weeds and the wheat will be allowed to grow together. The sorting of wheat and weeds can wait. Now, this story does not pretend that the weeds are just fine. There will be a necessary sorting, but it can wait until the harvest when the farmer can truly tell what is weed and what is wheat.

So it may be that our own wheat and our own weeds need to be allowed space to grow together. The weeds are still weeds and recognized as such. They will be sorted. But in the meantime the wheat will grow, and our ground may become a fertile field that produces a beautiful harvest, despite our weeds. Please be clear, if your shadows take you into ways of being that are harmful to yourself or to others, it's absolutely vital to get help to face the reality of this and to find ways to emerge into light. This practice is definitely not about condoning any out-of-control behaviour. But it is to do with being real about our flip-sides, our struggles and our darknesses.

Writing in the Sand

In the Jesus tradition there has always been a brilliant belief that, whatever the nature of our shadows, there is always the possibility for healing and hope. There's a powerful story in which a woman is dragged in front of Jesus who is teaching in the Temple precinct. In line with the law of Moses, the woman is threatened with stoning for committing adultery. The religious leaders ask Jesus what he thinks should be done with her, trying to catch him out, looking to expose his perceived liberal attitude towards the law. There's no mention of the man involved. On any level this is rough justice. In a dramatic scene, Jesus bends down and writes in the sand. He then stands and says, 'Let anyone among you who is without sin be the first to throw a stone at her.' Slowly the crowd begins to disperse. The Gospel writer finishes the story with sparse brilliance:

. . . and Jesus was left alone with the woman standing before him. Jesus straightened up and said to her, 'Woman, where are they? Has no one condemned you?' She said, 'No one, sir.' And

Jesus said, 'Neither do I condemn you. Go your way, and from now on do not sin again.'[1]

This story is full of wisdom for learning about handling our shadow. The attitude of the accusers highlights how interested we can be in exposing other people's shadows as a way of ignoring or suppressing our own. Jesus' pause and his writing in the sand suggest the importance of reflecting on what is going on, rather than jumping to an easy conclusion. The dwindling crowd reminds us that we all have shadows – without exception. And Jesus' words to the unnamed woman are full of compassion: 'Neither do I condemn you.' Our shadows, however deep, are not reason for us to condemn ourselves or to be condemned. But he is also realistic about how we need to decide to live not from our shadow but from our light. 'Go your way, and from now on do not sin again.'

Befriend Your Shadow: A Practice

 One way into befriending your own shadow is to recognize what you condemn in others. The next time you feel angry with someone, reflect on what may be going on. Of course their behaviour may need addressing. But the point in the practice of *Befriend Your Shadow* is to turn the light quietly onto ourselves. Be curious. Is there something in this person that is actually present in similar form in me? How does that behaviour materialize in me? And how could I change for good?

Befriend Your Shadow is a vital step towards the hardest but perhaps most important befriending: to greet our passing.

---

1 John 8.9b–11. There is some doubt as to whether John wrote this story into his Gospel. Some believe that it was a story circulated orally, initially left out of any of the Gospels but later reckoned too important to ignore and inserted into the text of the Gospel of John. In or out, I agree – it's a stunning story that deserves our attention and devotion.

20

Greet Your Passing

TERMINAL VELOCITY

Apparently there's a moment
in every falling – they call it terminal velocity –
when you can drop no faster.

Time perhaps to cease
from spinning and twisting,
from fighting and resisting –
time instead to shape the fall into
a flight of intention
a dive into grace
a movement into your new existence?

So the next time you are falling
open your arms wide and
take
a
deep
breath;
look all around you
and sense what may be
opening up before you . . .

*Unless a grain of wheat falls into the earth and dies, it remains
just a single grain; but if it dies, it bears much fruit.*

A teaching of Jesus: John 12.24

Even Somehow Good?

If you watch TV or go to the cinema you will, most days, see a death. Of course this is usually far removed from the reality of an actual experience of death close at hand. Sometimes it's only the passing of a loved one that brings home to us the true nature of death and the questions it raises. For most of us, I suspect, there is somewhere deep down a quiet undercurrent of fear of death, an awkward reality against which we are ready to rage[1] but which we most usually cope with through leaving well alone. But there is perhaps a deeper truth about our death that means that we need not be so fearful of it.

Is it possible that our passing from this life might somehow be acceptable, in tune with the ways things need to be, and even somehow good? This may be the hardest practice of all, but to live a truly good and generous life it is, I think, essential. To be fully human, we need to prepare ourselves for making the greatest journey we will ever encounter after the journey into human life itself. And there may be a freedom that comes from sensing that our death will, through all its toughness, be part of a greater pattern. If we can learn to greet our passing, to befriend our death, we may be free to live without constraint now, not fearfully looking over our shoulder at whatever may be catching up with us.

Sitting in the Cave

The Desert Fathers and Mothers were the radical forerunners of the monastic life in the ancient Jesus tradition. Their lives of ascetic devotion to God took them deeply into the reality of death, its questions, its fears and its possibilities. The fourth-century Desert Father Evagrius is clear about the importance of greeting our passing:

---

1 As suggested so memorably by the poet Dylan Thomas.

Sit in your cell, collecting your thoughts. Remember the day of your death. See then what the death of your body will be; let your spirit be heavy, take pains, condemn the vanity of the world, so as to be able to live always in the peace you have in view without weakening.[2]

For Evagrius, the acceptance of our death, as tough as this may be (and Evagrius is clear that this will be a demanding route to take), is essential if we are to live in true peace now. I like the way that Evagrius is encouraging us to picture ourselves beyond death, remembering our death, looking back at it. He's already looking *beyond* the time of passing. In his wisdom there is already a sense of a bigger picture emerging.

This practice is a way into maturity. If we can become ready to let go at the right time of the life-force that seems most dear to us, we may be enabled to live lives that make a difference *now*. Get used to the possibility of the greatest letting go, and some of the things we cling to now will lose their hold on us. Jesus' famous saying about the grain of wheat needing to fall into the earth to die carries great wisdom. The fruit that will emerge may be unimaginable to the seed. How could such a descent into loss produce anything good? And yet of course, as we know with the insight of a wider perspective, it will.

The idea of presence is particularly helpful here. The Gospel of Matthew closes with Jesus saying, 'I am with you always, to the end of the age.'[3] The entire sweep of his life and its events can be seen in this light. His life was, is and always will be one huge *I am with you*. This is what theologians call the Incarnation. God is with us. We are not alone. And the One who made this promise took the same route himself. The Passion – the story of Jesus' suffering and

---

2 Benedicta Ward SLG (trans.), *The Sayings of the Desert Fathers: The Alphabetical Collection*, Kalamazoo: Cistercian, 1975, p. 63.

3 Matthew 28.20.

death – is a story of descent with no guarantee of ascent to follow. But his acceptance of the falling into death opened up the space for the unimaginable ascent to burst into being.

Arc of Life

We are people of earth. From dust and ash we came and to dust and ash our bodies will return. So it seems ridiculous to live as if this will not happen. But this is what so many of us do. We plot our lives on an ever-rising trajectory. But life is actually more like an arc, appearing, rising, falling and disappearing. This is not a bad thing. The falling (the second half of life) can reveal within us far deeper qualities, greater achievements and stronger love than we could have imagined was possible when we were in the rising period (the first half of life).

A mature acceptance of the reality of our death will help us to deal with all the disappointments that inevitably come our way. If we are blessed with good health it remains very possible to enjoy our bodies, even through the inevitable changes that will come. And when some illness comes our way, our practice of letting go may enable us to live with some of the tougher aspects of that experience. As demanding as they are, these seeming setbacks may be just more steps in our quest to become the truly good human beings that we sense we are meant to be, bringing goodness to the world around us.

Greet Your Passing: A Practice

 So I wonder what might happen if we begin to see preparation for our death as a key task for a good life? *Greet Your Passing* is about accepting the one-day-reality of our death. It's also about nurturing an openness towards the evolving, passing and changing nature of life now.

Taking the advice of the Desert Fathers and Mothers, the practice of *Greet Your Passing* is a daily call to *remember the death of your body*. Here's a meditation to help you into the practice:

As you prepare to sleep, lie on your back for a few minutes.
Place your hands on your heart in a gesture of gratitude.
Give thanks for another day of life.
Make a prayer for a good passing from this life through death.
Ask for strength and peace for the journey whenever that day
    may come –
And for joy for whatever may unfold.

21

Discover Your Thankfulness

HOLY GROUND

Even the most mundane moment
in the most ordinary time
in a season of dullness
may be holy ground where
bushes crackle and burn
old rhythms are heard
new names are given
and lost songs resound.

So when you see me in the street
taking off my shoes
removing my hat
falling to my knees
and opening my hands, please

join me and
take off your shoes
remove your hat
fall to your knees
and open your hands, for

this may be holy ground where
bushes crackle and burn
old rhythms are heard
new names are given
and lost songs resound.

Even the most mundane moment
in the most ordinary time
in a season of dullness
may be holy ground.

Then (Jesus) ordered the crowds to sit down on the grass. Taking the five loaves and the two fish, he looked up to heaven, and blessed and broke the loaves, and gave them to the disciples, and the disciples gave them to the crowds. And all ate and were filled; and they took up what was left over of the broken pieces, twelve baskets full.

From the life of Jesus: Matthew 14.19–20

Swallows Low Over the Water

A blur of dark blue, white and a splash of red. A pair of swallows swoop low over the Aune estuary, flying through the wooden posts that mark the route of the road when it's covered at high tide, diving for insects low over the water. Their undulating flight is one of the quiet summer wonders of this part of the natural world. Following the movement through binoculars is almost impossible. Better just to see with the naked eye, to marvel, and to laugh along with the joyful nature of their work. Their flight is full of thankfulness. And when we begin to recognize this we may come to see that the flight of the swallows is just one shining tip of a whole cosmos that seems to be giving thanks. Thankfulness is bursting out from every wing tip, every mottled pebble, from every bright flower, every welcome breeze, and even from every hard rain.

The practice of *Discover Your Thankfulness* brings together something from all the practices that we've explored up to this point – practices of earth and body, of stillness and movement, and of descent. It's one of the most effective practices for helping us to reshape ourselves, so that we can run over rocks, and bring good to the world. I want to suggest that thankfulness is part of our natural state of being. It's waiting within us, longing to surface. But the demands of life can suppress our thankfulness, constrict it, even flatten it. So we may need to (re)discover our thankfulness, release it and nurture it. We need to discover how to become thankful people again!

The Examen: Wild Flowers at the Roadside

The practice of the Examen is at the heart of a particular strand of the Jesus tradition, Ignatian spirituality. A series of both demanding and freeing practices has emerged from the life and work of St Ignatius Loyola (1491–1556), founder of the Jesuits (the Society of Jesus). The daily Examen is a key element of the Ignatian path, a prayerful reflection of the past day's events and the possibilities of the day to come. Here's my own take on the Examen, including some simple gestures. The practice lends itself well to be done at a boundary point of the day – an obvious time is before sleep:

1. Open yourself to the possibility of God's presence. (Open your hands.)[1]
2. Let events from the day play back to you. Give thanks for the good things. (Hold your hands to your heart.)
3. Let the emotions that you have experienced today play back to you.[2] Be curious about why you felt this. (Hands held to stomach.)
4. Let one element or moment from the day become a prayer. (Hands to lips.)
5. Look toward to tomorrow with hope. Let a prayer for the new day form. (Open hands again.)

---

1 See Practices 8, 'Slow into Stillness', and 9, 'Find the Stillpoint' for more on opening up to divine presence.

2 See Practice 19, 'Befriend Your Shadow' for more on becoming aware of our emotions.

Thankfulness is the vital pivot upon which the practice of Examen rests. It's the doorway from one day (however tough or beautiful that day may have been) into the next day. It grounds us in the present moment. If you practise the Examen for a while you'll begin to find yourself giving thanks during the day, not just at the end of it. Thankfulness will move from being just an act of memory into an act of present engagement. It will start to become an unconscious stance of your life. You will become a person *who is* thankful, rather than just someone who sometimes remembers to say 'thank you'!

However, the Examen is also demanding, suggesting that not all may be as we would wish it to be. One of the disquieting things that this practice soon reveals, particularly in the third step, is how we can seem to be dominated by disappointment rather than thankfulness, by dis-ease rather than serenity. And these unhelpful and unattractive emotions can easily begin to characterize us. But the practice also reveals the joyful truth that we don't need to be held in those negative places. We have a choice. We can discover our thankfulness. And however the day has gone, there will almost certainly be a growing number of happenings, encounters, moments and surprises for which we will find ourselves giving thanks – a small strip of wild flowers at the edge of the toughest road.

Miracle of Thankfulness

Jesus taught and lived out from a state of thankfulness. The famous story, told in various guises in the Gospels, of his miraculous feeding of thousands of people with just a few loaves and fishes is rooted in thankfulness. However you read the story – as a physical miracle of a few loaves and fish becoming food for thousands, or as an equally magnificent and unlikely sociological miracle of people sharing their own food with others – this is a miracle of thankfulness.

At the end of a tiring day of teaching and crowd control the Disciples seem aware only of their own limited presence. Jesus, taking the Disciples into something that looks rather like a simple practice of Examen, lifts their awareness to the presence of God, as he looks up in a gesture of openness to a greater Presence. He then receives the (apparently meagre) gift of loaves and fish with gratitude, blessing the food. The Disciples, surely full of doubt, begin to share out the few fish and loaves with those at the front of the crowd, their emotions engaged in a tussle between astonishment and disbelief. The story unfolds. Not only are all fed but there are basketfuls of food left over – a detail of abundance that will form a starting point of wondrous possibility for the Disciples and future disciples for days, months, years and centuries to come. Thankfulness changes us; thankfulness changes the world.

Discover Your Thankfulness: A Practice

Commit to doing the Examen each night for a week as you prepare to go to sleep. Practise the simple rhythm of five steps. Notice what it does to you. See how you wake up each morning. Be curious about how the new day unfolds, and how your path over the rocks begins to open up. *Discover Your Thankfulness!*

PRACTICES OF ASCENT

From scarcity towards abundance: choosing generosity

Some places seem to offer a gift of restoration. For a week in summer this beach on the Isle of Mull became the mat for our yoga, stillness and prayer.

Human beings have an astonishing capacity to come back from whatever seems to be the most hopeless of situations. We are amazingly resilient, hungry for life, and capable of extraordinary ascent. With this comes new energy and possibility of bringing good to the world. But some of the less welcome patterns of thought and behaviour that come our way in the time of descent can prove to have a stubborn hold on us.

Descent can squeeze us into a mindset of scarcity. But ascent may come as we learn to be generous. However deep or far we feel we may have fallen, a time for ascent will one day reveal itself. This series of practices aims to enable us to find our way back onto our feet when we have fallen into the dark gaps between life's rocks and hard places. We haven't rushed from these gaps. We've seen that it's vital to stay with the descent. But when the grace-filled moment for ascent comes we must be ready to give ourselves to it with equal intensity. It awaits us. After the falling, the rising.

The season connected with these Practices of Ascent is Eastertide. The ascent that follows Good Friday and Holy Saturday is totally unexpected, but truly astounding. In the story of the resurrection, everything changes, everything becomes possible!

22

Welcome Today

SACRED MESSENGER

Out on the bay, an unsettling as
one gleaming fin breaks the surface,
then the curved black back. Close now

the great animal's eye holds mine
with acceptance and questioning;
could I even say with love?

Perhaps the bearer of a gift, a sacred messenger,
urging us to recover our primordial path,
to dive into the depths of our belonging

then break the surface of all that keeps
us diminished and fearful. And so
to rise, joyful.

*As they came near the village to which they were going, Jesus
walked ahead as if he were going on. But they urged him strongly,
saying, 'Stay with us, because it is almost evening and the day is
now nearly over.' So he went in to stay with them. When he was at
the table with them, he took bread, blessed and broke it, and gave
it to them. Then their eyes were opened, and they recognized him;
and he vanished from their sight.*

From the life of Jesus: Luke 24.28–31

Dial Set to 92

The radio remains one of the great morning rituals, a way into the new day. In the bedroom, bathroom and kitchen, on the commute to work and online wherever we are, radio still matters. I mature slowly, so it took me a few decades to get (BBC) Radio 3. Then, in my 40s, a slow epiphany. Its genius is its understated, geeky love for the music. Like any great music radio it's *all about the music*. So here the dial is set to 92. From Breakfast on 3 until Jazz on 3, Late Junction or World on 3 it's part of the soundtrack to my day.

A significant upward step on the ascent from our falls between life's rocks is the realization that every new day already carries with it all that we need – perhaps even all that we desire. From early morning until late night, it's all here waiting for you. It just needs your attention, your love, your presence. The practice of *Welcome Today* builds on our attention to the moment[1] by seeing each new day as full of possibility – and seeing the *arc of the whole day* as being a particular gift. So the movements from sleep into waking, from stillness into action, from work into play, from fasting into feasting, and eventually from movement back into rest (so in my case right through from Breakfast on 3 to Late Junction) become the settings for a truly human life, bringing good to ourselves, to those around us and to the wider world.

Under the Day's Skin

Of course we spend a lot of time thinking about tomorrow. Or about some future beyond tomorrow. And tomorrow and its possibilities have their place. They will need our attention when they come. But today is the great gift! The change in thinking that this requires is a challenge, but it is a key unlocking a door to a new world (or actually, to the world as it truly is). The big thing is not to treat today as a step towards what you are hoping for some day

---

1 See Practice 11, 'Be Here, Be Now'.

in the future, but to accept that this day already contains the seeds of all that you hope for. This is it! Now of course *this particular today* may not feel special. In fact it might be important that it does not feel special. We need to allow ourselves to be drawn under the skin of the day and into its earthy mystery. In the religious way of seeing the world this is about understanding that the divine comes to us in the life we live and encounter each day. The sacred is not to be grasped for. God is not out of reach, but rather here with us now in the most ordinary of happenings, in the most mundane of elements, in the most surprising of encounters, in the today.

Luke tells a wonderful story of the unexpected gift of today as part of his wider narrative of the resurrection of Jesus. Two of his followers, devastated at his execution and the apparent destruction of his movement, are fleeing from the city of Jerusalem to their home in the village of Emmaus.[2] As they walk, a stranger joins them on the road. A long conversation follows as they journey through the late afternoon. The day is in descent and night falling as they come to their destination. The unknown companion is invited to stay the night. He agrees, and as he breaks bread for the evening meal and gives thanks for the food they recognize that he is Jesus. One of the many interesting aspects of the story is that it is in the breaking of bread – an ordinary, daily action within the culture – that Jesus is recognized, and the divine possibility is glimpsed. The today that had dawned in despair became the setting for a new hope. And so each one of our todays is full of possibility.

A New Centre of Gravity

This is not about desperately trying to cram in a whole lifetime's experiences into a day, but about being fully present to the day and engaging with it. This is (quietly) one of the most radical steps

---

2 There are different theories regarding the exact location of Emmaus, placing it between 7 and 18 miles from Jerusalem.

we could take as we seek to bring goodness to the world. For if we learn to *Welcome Today* we will in turn become a small gift to those around us and to the world. We may even be able to live out the ancient calling that Jesus embraced and taught – to *love God and love neighbour*. Whenever we let the day be a gift, our centre of gravity moves from future objectives or past hurts to whatever or whoever is in front of us. We learn how to give attention to the person we are talking with, to the place in which we find ourselves, or to the task that we are engaged in, not looking (in reality or metaphorically) over their shoulder.

Welcoming the day may also help us to avoid being overwhelmed by the wider world's problems and challenges. If we welcome the day as it comes to us we'll find ourselves giving attention to the issues as they present themselves to us where we are, and that focus means that our actions will make a difference. The big picture continues to matter. But we are more likely to make a difference if we focus on doing something where we are today, rather than shelving the task for some imagined clear day.

Welcome Today: A Practice

 This stance of *Welcome Today* is about receiving each day as being full of possibility. One way into this stance is to create a simple ritual that you can repeat each morning, a conscious statement of your intention to welcome the gift of today. You could play a piece of music[3] that takes you into this stance, incorporate a particular move or gesture into your 'Come home to your body'[4] practice, or perhaps use a saying or prayer at the start of the day. This works very well as a complementary action to the Examen[5] practice of thankfulness usually done at the end of the

---

3 Find your own favourite. Elbow's song 'One Day Like This' works well for me.
4 See Practice 1, 'Come Home to Your Body'.
5 See Practice 21, 'Discover Your Thankfulness'.

day. Thankfulness and welcome have, in their humility, a strength that is much greater than any of their many opposites.

Today is a gift. Today is when the world is changed. *Welcome Today!*

23

Be Curious

SATURDAY'S TEAM SHEET

Rohr

Bianchi   O'Donohue   Nouen   Van

J'Norwich   Francis   Theodora

Jonsi   T'Avila   Vincent

E'Trinity
J'Cross
Stipe
Dillard
Collumcille
Br Roger
Coupland

Ask, and it will be given to you; search, and you will find; knock, and the door will be opened for you. For everyone who asks receives, and everyone who searches finds, and for everyone who knocks, the door will be opened.

A teaching of Jesus: Matthew 7.7–8

Who are Your Wisdom Teachers?

Who are your gurus? Your wise men and wise women? Your wisdom teachers? The good news is that, when we realize that we have such companions, whatever the question or dilemma we face, we don't have to make up the answer. We just have to be open to the collective wisdom of earth, creatures, people and the divine – ready for the wisdom that is ready for you. I'm calling this practice *Be Curious*. We need to cultivate a curious way of life. And however young or old we are, and however experienced or inexperienced we might be, it's vital to keep on learning. We need to become adept at sensing and receiving the wisdom which is offering itself to us.[1]

So this is (in part) about being open to the wisdom of the ancients, the experts, the brilliant ones. The players on 'Saturday's team sheet' are some of my wise guides, and I'm constantly inspired by them and others like them. It was tough picking the eleven for this Saturday, and dare I say, the bench is looking particularly strong. The wisdom can come in various ways: I like to work to music. Most of the music I choose to write to is wordless. But I love writing in the company of REM. The imagination and wisdom of their music keeps on nurturing me, encouraging me to continue on my path, even when writing feels like shoving a very large animal up the stairs. I just hope that I've imbibed their spirit, and not too many of their lines.

Surprising Sources

There's a whole storehouse of expert wisdom from which we can draw. But there's also great wisdom in the seemingly humble event, the inexperienced person and the surprising source. In his rule for the monastic life St Benedict makes clear that monks are to be

---

1 See Practice 3, 'Close-up (Terra Divina)' for practices to enable us to encounter the gift and wisdom of the natural world.

honoured in terms of the date of entry to the community, their virtues and the judgement of the abbot.[2] This is about valuing experience that leads to wisdom taking shape in good lives. But Benedict also urges the abbot of the monastery to make sure that the youngest and newest members of the community are heard before any big decision is taken that affects the community.[3] So wisdom transcends all our boundaries. And wisdom is not the same as knowledge. This is why we should not be surprised if we occasionally encounter someone with great knowledge (and perhaps many qualifications to prove it) but who seems to act with little wisdom! And why we should pay close attention to the un-educated, unknown or unrecognized person who is living from a place of deep wisdom.

It's important too to look beyond the limits of our tradition, our field or our discipline. So make sure that you are in the conversation spaces where your contemporaries are. I'm learning every day through being in the market places of ideas that are the social media. One of the most exciting arenas I've come across recently for the sharing of collective wisdom is the TED[4] movement, with its tag-line 'Ideas worth spreading'. It's inspiring to see people across the world so willing to engage in the sharing of wisdom for the twenty-first century.

Wisdom and the Feminine

The teaching of Jesus conveys a strong belief that we *will* find the wisdom that we need if we are serious in our search for it. 'Ask,' Jesus says, 'and it will be given to you; search, and you will find; knock, and the door will be opened for you.' For Jesus, the source of this wisdom is 'your Father in heaven'. If we search diligently

2 *The Rule of St Benedict in English*, ed. T. Fry, Collegeville, MN: Liturgical Press, 1982, ch. 63, 'Community Rank'.

3 *The Rule of St Benedict*, ch. 3, 'Summoning the Brothers for Counsel'.

4 www.ted.com.

and faithfully, the divine wisdom for life will be ours. Some truths, like many places, open themselves up slowly[5] so the search will require persistence. Wisdom is to be sought, but need not be chased. So let the wisdom that you need find you. Then allow the wisdom to shape you.

There's an interesting aspect of the teaching on wisdom from the ancient Jewish tradition, in which wisdom is thought of as being feminine. Jesus himself taught this: 'wisdom is vindicated by her deeds'.[6] Perhaps this emphasis emerged from long-lived evidence that wisdom is particularly discovered through what might be seen as women's experiences – through suffering, through nurturing others, through sharing stories, and through intuition. Or perhaps it came about simply because men have seemed so often to act from the many opposites of wisdom! Wisdom, after all, cannot be won by the kind of power games often associated with men. Rather, true wisdom has a mysterious and tender quality that means it must be treated with reverence. One of the greatest and earliest basilicas (sanctuaries or houses) of the Church was dedicated to the Holy Wisdom of God – the Hagia Sophia[7] in contemporary Istanbul. To this day it's a reminder to us to continue in our search for Holy Wisdom.

---

5 Ian Adams, *Cave Refectory Road: Monastic rhythms for contemporary living*, London: Canterbury Press, 2010, p. 84.

6 Matthew 11.19.

7 For centuries a magnificent church building, Hagia Sophia was converted into a mosque in 1453, and since 1935 has been a museum. The building (actually the third church building erected on the site, built between 532 and 537) remains, of course, a stunning example of early church architecture.

Be Curious: A Practice

 The collective wisdom of the cosmos does not belong to us (or to anyone). It is bigger and deeper and wider than all of us. It's greater than the philosopher writing it, the artist painting it, the teacher teaching it, or the politician arguing it. If there's any wisdom in *Running Over Rocks,* I trust that as well as emerging thoughtfully from my own experiences it will transcend my own shortcomings, and reflect and draw from the greater wisdom around me. Wisdom must be always be passed on, so that someone else can take it to the next place on its journey.

Here's a practice of *Be Curious* that draws on the wisdom of the famous Israelite king Solomon, as offered to the world in an ancient book attributed to him and found in the Jewish scriptures. The wisdom of the Book of Proverbs is earthy and spiritual, detailed and epic, surprising and disturbing. There are 31 chapters in the wisdom book of Proverbs, so it's straightforward enough to work with the chapter with the same number as the date in the month. Slowly read the chapter, being alert to its wisdom for you, and let it do its work on you. As I write this passage it's the 15th of the month. Here's wisdom from Proverbs 15: 'A soft answer turns away wrath, but a harsh word stirs up anger.' This is wisdom that reaches out to us from 4,000 years ago. It remains as vital and insightful now as it was when first shared. Look for the wisdom you need – it's coming towards you. *Be Curious!*

24

Find Your Deep Flow

RIVER FLOWING

You may sense the movement of a river
flowing around you; you may not know
its source its course its depth, nor
the surprise of the great poet's unfolding
nor yet the ocean into which it will one day
emerge – but it is there all the same

waiting for you to immerse yourself
in its promise, so that you may become
a gift to all, a fast flowing stream
carrying you out onto the open sea
of your life, an undertow of love
for the world.

*The kingdom of heaven is like a merchant in search of fine pearls;
on finding one pearl of great value, he went and sold all that he
had and bought it.*

A parable of Jesus: Matthew 13.45–46

Why are You Here?

There is no other in the cosmos quite like you, and your exact likeness will not be here again. So imagine for a moment the impact
you want to have for good on the world. Why are you here, in this
place, at this time? We are each privileged and burdened with the
unique reality of our own lives. But it's easy to lose our bearings,
our focus and our sense of the direction of our own possibility.
Sometimes we need a compass to bring us back on course.

Gail Adams is a life coach and mentor, running the See:Change
project.[1] Some of her insightful work is around developing metaphors and ideas to help us locate this sense of our own calling – to
get in touch with the person we each know we need to be, bringing good to the world. She calls this quest our *Deep Flow* and I'm
grateful for her insights which have helped shape this stance in
Running Over Rocks. *Deep Flow* is not just about your role in life,
although hopefully your role or job will be one way in which you
can express your *Deep Flow*. We are truly happy only when we are
having a positive effect on our family, friends, communities, our
environment and the wider world. Interestingly and rightly, something as important as this is not easy to define. It has a mysterious
quality that it is vital to respect and treat with tenderness.

Into Deep Flow

One of the ways that Gail begins to work with people to introduce the possibility of *Deep Flow* looks like this. She gathers people
around a large box of sand, with a river flowing through a landscape painted onto the box. Everyone is invited to choose one
of a number of small sailing boats and then to place their boats
somewhere in the box, intuitively sensing the place where they
find themselves at this time. Some always place their boats some
distance from the river, and talk about being lost, far from where

1 For more on discovering your Deep Flow: Gail Adams – www.theseechange.info.

they know they want to be. Some say they are in the shallows of the river, and speak about having a sense that they are somewhere in the right place, but perhaps losing momentum, spinning in an eddy. Some place themselves on the sand at the river's edge, and talk about being beached or stuck. Sometimes people place their boats up a creek, and talk about having been on the river but then somehow having lost their way.

And occasionally some are in the deep, fast-flowing centre of the river – the place of *Deep Flow*. Here people talk about having begun to find themselves, about discovering what they had always wanted to become and beginning to live that way.

The invitation is now made to begin to move our boats closer in the direction of the river and towards its deepest flowing centre. We then wonder together what that move might look like in real life. The important thing here is not to try to make a huge step from land to centre of river, but to begin to practise taking small steps in that direction. Every decision, every challenge, every day is another opportunity to begin to move in this direction. We'll also soon realize that every decision, every challenge, every day can also bring a subtle (or not-so-subtle) pressure to abandon our desire to live in *Deep Flow*. The choice will be ours.

The Pearl Worth Everything

Jesus tells a series of vivid parables about what he calls the kingdom of heaven – that better world now-and-always, where everything good flourishes, with you and me and everything learning to be truly ourselves. In one of these parables he describes this blissful state of being as a pearl of great value for which a merchant sold everything that he had in order to own it. This pearl, says the wise teacher, is worth giving everything for. So there will be a cost to discovering and then living within and out from your *Deep Flow*. Some things will have to be left behind or declined if we are to live our calling. Sometimes we may need to take decisions to stay in our *Deep Flow* that make little sense on other scales of measurement. Actions that come from a commitment to your calling may seem strange to others. In terms of financial security, of public recognition or generally accepted wisdom, our calling may seem foolish, indulgent or hopeless. But your *Deep Flow* is a gift, and to run over rocks you need to find it, move towards it, and stay in it!

Find Your Deep Flow: A Practice

It's important to remember that only you can be you. So be you! Whatever your background, whatever your tradition, whatever your stage in life, we each have a reason to be here, a contribution to make a better world, and what I believe is a unique calling. Of course your calling will have similar characteristics to that of many others. But only you can enable that calling to come together with the mix of desire, passion, need, place and timing that are unique to you, to make a difference for good. The process of finding our *Deep Flow* requires close attention. The nature of our *Deep Flow* may evolve, but it always seems to have the same overall direction. Some of the details may change, but the impulse at the heart of your *Deep Flow* gets ever stronger.

One way to *Find Your Deep Flow* is to reflect on the moments, times or seasons when you have felt that you were truly being yourself in who you have been, and in what you have been doing. So ask yourself these questions: Where was I when I sensed that I was being who I was meant to be, doing what I was meant to do? What was the essence of that experience? And what's the first small step I could take in a new direction to access that same way of being now? These may be some of the most important questions that you will ever ask – questions seeking the pearl of great value. The pearl worth giving everything for!

25

Creative You

HAMMER, CHISEL AND FILE

In a garden enclosed
primal figures of
stone and bronze
trace the roughed edges
the scooped hollows
and the graced curves
of all our ages.

The sculptor has long left
this sanctuary,
but despite that dark leaving
her spirit remains here,
and also her tools. So

I put on the working shirt
that hangs on the door, pick up
a hammer, a chisel and a file
and move towards the
rough stone block
that awaits me.

You are the light of the world. A city built on a hill cannot be hid-
den. No one after lighting a lamp puts it under the bushel basket,

117

*but on the lampstand, and it gives light to all in the house. In the
same way, let your light shine before others, so that they may see
your good works and give glory to your Father in heaven.*

A teaching of Jesus: Matthew 5.14–16

Dancing in the Stream (of Something Beyond Us)

Bliss. Apparently I have a smile on my face when I'm painting.
Like a child engrossed in play. When we get deep into the creative
act something interesting happens. We find ourselves dancing in
the stream of something beyond us. Creativity is one of the ways
in which we flourish as human beings, holding us when we are
in descent, and releasing us into ascent when the opportunity
appears. To be creative is to step into our own mystery, and to sense
our deep connection to the sacred. So creativity truly matters!

It's an amazing thing when our general impulse towards creativity finds a focused action in which it can be expressed. For some
people this direction feels really clear. I was, they say, born to play
the violin (or paint, or bake or whatever). But for many of us the
creative path feels much less familiar. We might get occasional tan-
talizing glimpses of the path, but it can feel as if we've completely
lost the trail. Through lack of nurture or just from the busy-ness of
life we can misplace or lose our capacity to be creative. When this
becomes a cultural thing, passed through the generations, it may
take some remarkable intervention – perhaps from a particularly
inspiring teacher – to bring about change. Our creativity is often
suppressed in us as children or as young people, pushed way down
to a point where as adults we have lost not just the skills we may
have once shown naturally, but perhaps even more tragically the
natural confidence to give ourselves to *any* experiment that might
lead to a line on paper, a tune being sung, or a recipe being created. So don't be surprised if your way back to your creative path
feels painful and exhilarating! The practice of *Creative You* is the

vital work of locating (or relocating) and stepping into our creative path.

Participating in the Healing of All Things

In the Judaeo-Christian tradition the act of creativity is one of the chief characteristics of the nature of God. The tradition says that whenever we discover our creative impulse we are resonating with something of the ancient-and-forever life of the divine, participating in the constantly evolving nature of existence and the universe. To play the violin, to paint and to bake (or to design, craft, teach or whatever) may be to participate in the healing of all things. To imagine something new and shape it *in any field of human activity* can be a creative act. The rabbi Jesus, formed in this tradition, called people to bring the light of their creativity to the world: *let your light shine before others.*[1] Of course, how else can the world be changed? Don't hide your light – let it shine!

So make it your goal to discover (or recover) your creative path. In my experience most people have a sense deep down of what that might be. It can, however, be excruciatingly painful to own this truth because creative work of any kind requires us to put ourselves on the line. It's a demanding thing to put our creativity in front of others, and to own the creative name (artist, gardener, baker, painter, chef or poet). It's tough to go through the processes of doubting ourselves, of falling and of (apparent) failure, of exposing something of our inner being in whatever we create. This is the painful nature of the creative life.

Only You See the World this Way

The creative path requires courage. Some creatives already in your field will be gracious and encouraging to you. Others may be less

---

1 Matthew 5.16a.

so. But persist! The demanding path into creativity will turn out to be an amazing road to freedom for you, bringing goodness to the world around you. And we, of course, can choose how we respond to the work of others. We can choose to encourage them, and to be inspired and energized by their work. Or we can choose to nurture resentment and even jealousy. Beware the latter – it will only serve to demean us and diminish our own capacity for creativity.

You are unique, not just because you are talented (which in some area of creativity you certainly are or could become so) but because you have a unique viewpoint. Only you can see the world the way you do. Others will share a similar outlook, have a similar view, work in a similar way – but only you can see the world exactly as you do, and only you can create something unique in collaboration with the world that you see. This is such a vital concept for any artist or creative person. *Your* creativity truly matters! And if the work is not done by you it will not be gifted to the world. This is really helpful if you know what it's like to see someone else's brilliant work and feel as if *I could never do that*. You are right – you could never do *that* work quite like the person who has done it. No-one can. What matters is that you take the creative path that is calling *you*, and create what you are meant to create.

Creative You: A Practice

Creative You is a practice for the hard but vital work of rediscovering your creative path. It's the shaping of a ritual for entering into your creativity. The detail of the ritual you create will be very personal to you. Whatever you choose, make the ritual simple and meaningful to you. This is how the ritual looks for me:

- put on your creative clothing (my overalls work for me this way)

- put your music on (or turn it off)
- shut the door (or open the door)
- prepare the space to reflect and encourage creativity
- touch or hold the object that reminds you of your creative core
- let the stillness produce your first mark (it will come)
- break the creative act into small actions: draw a first line, play a first chord, pick the first ingredient
- trust the process, nothing is wasted
- don't discard work, but keep on layering it.

It's vital not to let the lack of the 'proper' materials or setting hold you back. A 'proper' studio, workshop, kitchen or garden would be great. But don't let their absence or presence hold you back. Work with the materials you have, in the place that you have been given. And do something every day. Keep turning up – and discover the *Creative You*!

26

Live with Momentum

A NEW DAY

6am: the dawn of a new day
and the stillness is releasing movement.
A mist on the Aune estuary
settled over yesterday's tides.
Now shafts of sunlight shimmer on the water
opening up the possibilities of a new day.
Birds shake their wings
and look up . . .

*The next day John again was standing with two of his disciples,
and as he watched Jesus walk by, he exclaimed, 'Look, here is the
Lamb of God!' The two disciples heard him say this, and they
followed Jesus. When Jesus turned and saw them following, he
said to them, 'What are you looking for?' They said to him, 'Rabbi'
(which translated means Teacher), 'where are you staying?' He
said to them, 'Come and see.'*

From the life of Jesus: John 1.35–39a

A Zen Koan

How do you move on from the top of a 100 foot pole? This was one
of the Zen koans put to us by the Catholic priest and Zen Roshi

Fr Robert Kennedy,[1] a speaker at a StillPoint[2] event in Oxford. The secret of a Zen koan or riddle lies within you. It's entered into intuitively rather than rationally. You don't think through an answer, you open yourself up to the koan's wisdom and allow it to work within you. The koan discovers you, and you receive it, whenever you are ready.

This particular koan brought something to the surface for me about momentum, and specifically about living with creative momentum in contrast to paralysed inactivity. There's a beautiful scene in Ang Lee's film *Crouching Tiger Hidden Dragon* in which the two main characters fight with swords while moving through a forest of tall bamboo. The bamboo has enough strength to hold them; but it flexes under their weight, allowing them to move. It's almost impossible to move safely from the top of a 100 foot pole if the pole you are clinging onto is a rigid wooden post. But if the pole is a giant bamboo pole, and if you have just moved onto this pole from another bamboo pole, both flexing as bamboos do, movement becomes possible, even full of energy and grace. The fight becomes a dance! The practice of *Live with Momentum* is about nurturing a sense of being light on our feet, of finding energy in engaging with whatever comes our way, and so learning to run over the rocks of the boulder field of the next season of our life.

Come and See: Movement Not Achievement

One of the many characteristics of the Jesus path that I have come to discover and love is that it is more about movement than achievement. Some spiritual traditions seem to picture the spiritual journey as a ladder towards success. As in a cosmic video game, with persistence and skill you get to the next level, killing

---

1 Robert Kennedy: www.kennedyzen.tripod.com.

2 StillPoint is a project of Ian Adams and Matt Rees, nurturing contemplative spirituality from within the ancient Jesus tradition and in engagement with other contemplative traditions: www.thestillpoint.org.uk.

the odd enemy or 'boss' on the way. Now of course there's some truth in that. The spiritual path needs our persistence and commitment. And those bosses – the things that threaten to dominate us or throw us off course – need to be encountered. But orthodox Christianity has always been wary of becoming a path of achievement only accessed by the truly hard-core disciple, or of becoming an esoteric destination only understood or reached by a particularly self-denying ascetic.

Rather, the ancient Jesus way sees itself as a path open to all, a daily call to live in the way of the One who says *Follow me* and who reassures us with *I am with you always*. The Gospel writer John recounts an early episode in which Jesus invites two disciples of the wild desert prophet John the Baptizer into his life of holy-and-earthed momentum. Intrigued by the man that their own teacher John has pointed to as 'the Lamb of God' they begin to walk behind him. He turns and asks them what they are looking for. They ask where he is staying – perhaps thinking that they will be able to sit with him there and discover more. His response is 'Come and see,' an invitation into movement, both on a simple physical level (as in 'Come and see where I am staying') and at a deeper level (as in 'Come and be with me on the road to discover what this life might look like'). The path of 'Come and see' is about movement rather than achievement. Rather than being learned through theory (as helpful as that can be), the spiritual life, the truly human life, is discovered in the momentum of living!

Fifteen Again, Freerunning

If I was fifteen again I'd love to learn the art of freerunning – a practice of negotiating the urban landscape that has emerged from the movement discipline of parkour.[3] This is a literal and exuberant *running over rocks* in the city. What a brilliant thing! To run and

---

3 A movement credited to David Belle, emerging from the teaching of his father Raymond Belle.

jump, to balance and slide in, on and through our physical sur-
roundings. To discover that walls, ramps and steps can be with us
rather than against us. To re-encounter concrete as a landscape of
possibility, energy and life. Freerunning harnesses the possibility
of continuous movement in an unpromising landscape. The practice of *Live with Momentum* encourages us to move in, through
and within the often unpromising landscape of our lives.

So how can we let the rocks that stand in our path become the
surfaces from which we can spring, where our energy finds new
momentum? How can we be like the freerunner, running, rolling,
and jumping off the city's paths and walls, so that the rocks we are
running over seem to reveal an inner elastic quality? This is a practice that requires a new perspective. However accomplished the
freerunner, the concrete is still tough and unforgiving material.
What changes is the perspective of the freerunner, who begins to
see how she can engage with this material so that it can absorb and
release her energy in a positive way rather than break her bones or
cut her skin. So this change of perspective is about learning to see
the tough things that come up as being potential sources of possibility rather than of danger. Like freerunning, this takes practice
and courage.

Live with Momentum: A Practice

 Unless you are a freerunner, *Live with Momentum*
will be for most of us a stance of imagination. It
nevertheless contains real possibility for how we
live each day. As a way in, take a walk near to where
you live or work. Begin to see the walls, paths,
ramps and roads as representing both the challenges and possibilities that are coming up for you. Imagine yourself running over
them, enjoying how they might give you new energy and direction.

Give yourself to this practice and you may find it shaping many
areas of your life. You may find yourself living more lightly to your

possessions, loosing your grip on whatever you used to think gave you security. You may find yourself welcoming opportunities to collaborate with others, and being willing to work on a number of different projects. You may even find that you can begin to take energy from the rocks – the tough things – that appear in your way. They may provide the momentum for a new direction that you would not otherwise have envisaged. Through it all you may find yourself nurturing a sense of your life as an ever-unfolding journey, full of possibility. So let's *Live with Momentum*!

27

Choose Abundance

BETWEEN FEAR AND GREED

This morning on the radio, they said
the markets bleed from black to red
and traders lurch between fear and greed
some making fortunes in pursuit of needs
must, eyeing the chance, working the odds –
and the trading floor is splattered in blood.

So what should we do? Accept this as the way
things must be. Or seek a better polarity?
To imagine what it might be like to arc
between hope and generosity, and so to mark
ourselves as truly human, to shape another path –
and exchange our loss for grace, at last.

*Give, and it will be given to you. A good measure, pressed down,
shaken together, running over, will be put into your lap; for the
measure you give will be the measure you get back.*

A teaching of Jesus: Luke 6.38

Mamka's Table

'Eat! Eat!' urges Mamka, mother of my university friend Mike.
We are sitting in her kitchen in Bradford, around a small table re-

plete with dishes of bread, meats and cheeses, bottles of beer and Stolichnaya vodka. Mamka (Mother) had come to England as a young woman in the aftermath of the Second World War, a Russian refugee fleeing unmentioned horrors. Here she met and married Mike's father Alexei, also a Russian refugee with a similarly hard story. In this northern English city they found a welcome among the small Russian community, and a place of peace and anonymity in which to build a new life for themselves and their children.

I remember Alexei saying little, smiling as he smoked. Mamka moved between fridge and table, continually bringing out more food as we ate. They were far from wealthy. But their hospitality was immense! At that kitchen table I was entering a promised land, tasting the milk and honey of abundance. I've reflected on that experience many times, on the generosity of these people, and how it shaped Mike, producing in him an instinctive generosity, a permanent sense of plenty, and a joyful immersion in the gift of the present moment.

Scarcity or Abundance?

One of the greatest challenges facing humanity at this time is the perceived lack of resources. There's not enough finance to pay for health care or pensions. We are running out of oil. The harvests aren't strong enough to cope with increasingly unusual weather patterns. The next wars will be over fresh water. All of these statements contain truth. But the reality is that there *are* enough resources – should we as human beings choose to share them, should we choose to amend the ways in which we use them, should we choose to live hopefully not fearfully. To choose abundance and generosity in this context of perceived shortage and scarcity is a tough calling. To reshape that context is even tougher. But the choosing and reshaping must be done!

We can understand the importance of finding (well-regulated and transparent) ways for people who have imaginative ideas for businesses to get in touch with people who have money to invest. But there's something deeply wrong when people make vast amounts by, in effect, *betting* on financial transactions. We can understand the need for (well-regulated and transparent) market places for commodities where growers can be put in contact with food distributors. But there is something deeply troubling when commodity traders make vast profits by buying up huge proportions of any particular foodstuff. What are we to do about this? Truth needs to be spoken to power, and right now there's a huge need for such truth to be spoken. With the proximity and effectiveness of social media we can all get involved in this truth-telling. It can't be left to politicians alone, as important as it is that we find politicians with the necessary courage and tenacity to do this. We have to get involved.

Ushpizin

The ascent practice of *Choose Abundance* brings good to us and good to the world around us. Resources are best shared, not hoarded. This is the teaching of Jesus who of course was steeped in the Jewish tradition of a good world full of the abundance of God. The ancient story of beginnings from that tradition[1] describes a world full of abundance, in which humanity has a role to care for the earth, and in which each element of creation is described as good. So it's not surprising to discover Jesus of Nazareth teaching abundance. 'Give, and it will be given to you. A good measure, pressed down, shaken together, running over.'[2] This is not a technique, not some pyramid scam to get rich or some prosperity gospel, but the simple insight that the more we share, the richer life becomes. It may be that Jesus is using the vivid imagery of a wine press, perhaps close by as he talks, seeing a full vat, messy but

---

1 Genesis chapter 1.
2 Luke 6.38a.

glorious, giving off the earthy aroma of the grapes being crushed, a promise of the gift of the wine to come.

The practice of abundance is of course wonderful when it's met with joy, with thanks – and with more abundance. But what are we to do if our attempts at living with abundance are met with indifference or advantage-taking? The film *Ushpizin*[3] tells the story of an Orthodox Jewish couple in Jerusalem trying to celebrate the festival of Sukkot while struggling to pay their bills amid the greater sadness of not being able to have a child. Due to the kindness of an anonymous donor they suddenly have enough money to pay their debts and to make the necessary arrangements to enjoy the festival. Their first action is to give away a tenth of the money that has come their way. Then they offer generous hospitality to some unexpected visitors. We are shocked when these guests (the *ushpizin*) turn out to be anything but gracious, trampling all over the generosity of their hosts. So it's humbling and beautiful to see the couple sticking with their commitment to abundance and generosity. Our commitment to abundance need not be knocked out of shape by the reaction of others. We can *Choose Abundance*!

Choose Abundance: A Practice

 One of the things that sustains the characters in *Ushpizin* in their commitment to abundance is their belonging to a community that is sharing this practice. The shared story of abundance can keep us generous when the tough times come. But the abundant life has to take shape in us, wherever we are today. Here's a three-step path into a practice of *Choose Abundance*:

1. Go regularly for a walk in your part of the natural world,[4] and let its reckless abundance – grass and flowers, air and water, soil

---

3 *Ushpizin*, 2004, Director: Gidi Dar; Writer: Shuli Rand.
4 See Practice 2, 'Walk the Good Earth'.

and sky – seep into you. Let the phrase 'It is good' repeat and resound in you.

2. Carry something with you that reminds you of your call to *Choose Abundance* – perhaps something given to you by someone else.

3. Every day, find a way to give something (away). You could make this an element of your daily Examen, linking this practice to the practice of *Discover Your Thankfulness*.[5]

---

5 See Practice 21, 'Discover Your Thankfulness'.

28

Live from Your Joy

JOYFUL POEM

one
  unsteady
even reticent
note, my child cry
seeking love.
With eyes closed
each breath deepening
I open my hands
and the one
note begins to find
others resounding, a song
emerging from the long silence.
Slowly I begin to spin around,
these arms as wings – then *faster*
they become translucent
like giant fireflies
dancing and not just mine
but many, hundreds, thousands
– and yours!
There are rings of light around us
as we dance, and the brilliant confluence
of Earth and Sky of Spirit and Body our
arms wide open, heads back singing –
we're throwing off all that holds us

down, and we're looking up
at the rain falling and we're
falling up into the sky,
laughing and
we are joy
and all is
one

I have said these things to you so that my joy may be in you, and that your joy may be complete.

A teaching of Jesus: John 15.11

Joy and Sorrow: Both

My son, my chosen and beloved
Share your wounds with your mother[1]

A week rarely goes by for me without the company of one version or another of Henryk Gorecki's Third Symphony (Symphony of Sorrowful Songs). One of the many interesting things about this powerful piece in three movements, based on searing experiences of abandonment and death, is a tangible sense of hope within sadness. Gorecki's sublime composition suggests that even death cannot hold back the human and divine spirit. It seems to suggest that joy may be deeper than both loss and finding, stronger than desolation or happiness. *Live from Your Joy* is a stance for all of life, a way to live that we can choose to pursue (however tough that may prove), and a stance that we can nurture with practice.

Joy is not based on things going right, or even well. Joy is not to be found on the other side of difficulty. I like the other side of

---

1 From Mary's lament for the crucified Jesus, Lamentation of the Holy Cross Monastery, the Lysagora collection, fifteenth century. Sung in the first movement of Gorecki's Symphony No. 3 (Symphony of Sorrowful Songs), Op. 36, 1976.

difficulty, of course – it's a good place to find ourselves – but that's not joy. The other side of difficulty is just a temporary state of being with things going as we would like them to. It's lovely, and I'd like more of it, but it's temporary. Nor is joy the opposite of sorrow. The kind of experiences that have produced in me a whole series of sorrowful poems are a necessary companion to joy! To truly experience joy we need to give ourselves to the experience of sorrow. Joy and sorrow are both about receiving life as it comes, accepting the darknesses, looking for the light, and sensing *in them both* the ultimate goodness of existence.

Joy is Close

The experience of the contemplative stream in the Jesus tradition is that joy is never far away; in fact joy is welling up within us if only we will allow it to grow, and let our joylessness diminish. It's a gift that we discover, not something we create. It can only be received, lived, and given away. And it can – and perhaps must – be found in the toughest of times and loneliest of places.

Towards the end of John's Gospel there's an intimate series of passages in which the writer describes Jesus speaking in very personal terms to the Disciples. These sayings in chapters 14–17 are probably gathered from a series of remembered conversations and teachings from the latter part of Jesus' public life, a period in which he is increasingly coming under threat. The immediate context in the Gospel is his imminent arrest and execution. So it might be surprising to find Jesus talking about joy. But his focus on joy is right here, woven through his forecast of being betrayed, his recognition of the Disciples' fearful bewilderment, his sense of the world's capacity for hatred, and his recognition of the pain and sorrow that will soon come to them all. 'I have said these things to you', says Jesus, 'so that my joy may be in you, and that your joy may be complete.' Joy is to be found alongside, and maybe even *within*, the sorrow that comes our way!

Hurt's Strange Attraction

How might we begin to live from our joy? For Jesus a life of joy emerges from an experience of *loving and being loved*. 'As the Father has loved me, so I have loved you: abide in my love.'[2] And this experience of love is not dependent on the love of another single human being (although that can be a beautiful way in which this love is mediated). The love that the teacher is referring to is the love that permeates all that exists (and the love within, and the love from, and love towards it): the good earth, the benevolent cosmos, and the community of God who is love. Joy emerges from our experience of loving and being loved.

So it will be hard to live from our joy if we have lost our capacity or memory for love, or if we persistently allow love's opposite – fear – to shape us.[3] I'm curious about the capacity we have for nurturing the opposites of joy. Hurt can have a strange attraction. We can find ourselves nurturing feelings of rejection, fuelling our hurt and suppressing our joy. So it's important to recognize that *Live from Your Joy* is about movement rather than achievement. It's a daily call to face and move in another direction away from fear, and to refuse to fuel our sense of being hurt. Some days this will feel very hard, other days it may all seem much more simple. So resolve each day to live from your joy, *as far as you can*. It's important not to be down on ourselves if we sense that this is slow to happen. And to recognize that our joy may not always conform to common perceptions. Joy can be quiet, sometimes experienced as just a slight shift within us. But there may well be moments too when joy bursts from us. When those exuberant moments come, let them loose!

---

2 John 15.9.
3 See Practice 50, 'Face Fear with Love'.

Live from Your Joy: A Practice

The practice of *Live from Your Joy* is, like many practices in *Running Over Rocks*, a combination of self-awareness and action.

Notice today what may be going on when you are *not* feeling joyful. Note the things that suppress your sense of joy. Pay particular attention to whatever you are resisting. There will be learning here. You may begin to see that you have some choice in allowing joy to surface.

Find something that helps you relocate the joy within you. For me that's often around music. I keep returning to *Kind of Blue* by Miles Davis, his extraordinary album from 1959. In the track 'Blue in Green' anything seems possible as Davis and friends improvise around the theme, surfing the joy (of green?) within the melancholy (of blue?). Find a piece of music – or something else – that opens up the path of joy for you. Let whatever you choose be your call into joy. Keep returning to it during the day. Let it break open the joy within you, and enable you to begin again to run over rocks.

PRACTICES OF POSSIBILITY

From loss towards grace: the art of looking up

I love painting on wood. One day I found a pallet washed up on the beach. 'Waves' is the result.

We've begun to grow practices that bring us home to our bodies and to the earth, and we've explored the amazing possibilities of stillness and movement. We have started to find practices to hold us in the times of descent and darkness, and we've begun to form practices for the ascent, whenever that may come. In this next series of practices we'll be forming practices of possibility that help us once again to look up, to widen our vision for life, and to step into the grace that is all around us.

When we are having to negotiate the difficult stuff that comes our way, to find our way through the rocks of the boulder field in front of us, our eyes are drawn down to where our feet may go. But to travel well, to run over rocks, we need to learn to size up these rocks in our peripheral vision, to see them as just part of a bigger picture. And to give our attention to what may be opening up on the horizon. Our attention is easily drawn to the rocks of our losses – while the world around is quietly burning with grace. Let's look up!

The seasons connected with these Practices of Possibility are Ascension and Pentecost. In these seasons the tradition begins to sense a new reality. The risen Jesus is understood as being close to every human person, through the presence of what theologians call God's Holy Spirit. In these seasons we are called to step into the flow of this Holy Spirit, to allow her to help us to rediscover the shape that we were always meant to be. To move from loss towards grace.

29

Choose Your Icons
(Become What You See)

FOREST OF FEARFUL FEARS

So dark the night
I slipped from the house
and took the track down to
the forest of fearful fears.

There I watched the trees
grow – feeding on the darkness,
packed close together
no living thing between.

I returned home cold before dawn
and lay in our bed,
shivering.

This morning I walked the track again, stopping
as the forest of fearful fears came into view.

The forest is a wood, surrounded by hills,
and a path runs through it.
An eagle is circling above.
And from here, beyond the wood,
I can see the sea
shining.

*Jesus took with him Peter and James and his brother John and led
them up a high mountain, by themselves. And he was transfigured
before them, and his face shone like the sun.*

From the life of Jesus: Matthew 17.1–2a

Kissing Icons

I strike a match, bring the flame to the candle, watch it take. I kiss
the icon. A kiss of greeting, recognition, humility, affection and,
yes, of love. And then a pause. How natural, how earthy, how good
this seems. This practice of the Orthodox Church has become part
of my life. But the place of icons has not always been accepted
or assured within Christianity, and that ambivalence continues
today. For over a hundred years in the time of the Byzantine empire it was a particularly divisive issue, surfacing in the frequently
bitter struggles that we know as the Iconoclasms of the eighth and
ninth centuries. I'm not going to recount those battles in detail
here.[1] Suffice to say that I'm for icons. I'm an iconophile, I'm an
iconodule, I love icons. I believe they are a great gift, simultane-
ously suggesting an alternative way to see the world for what it
truly is – an earthly-heavenly paradise – and opening ways for us
to live that paradise to the full wherever we are.

Images Shape the World

The visual image matters. And images and icons are all around us.
They shape our understanding and our instinct as human beings.
They shape us and they shape the world around us. We won't easily
forget the terrible images of the Twin Towers burning in New

---

1 A key argument against icons (or ikons) comes from adherence to the commandment in the Jewish scriptures to make no graven image of the divine. The counter-argument
begins by suggesting that in the coming of the Christ into the world as the man Jesus the
image of God has already and dramatically been offered to the world, and that to *not* write
or pray with icons would be to forget and dishonour this greatest of icons.

York on 9/11. There's no doubt that those darkly 'iconic' pictures changed the way we think about ourselves and about the complex world and our place in it. Images change perceptions within society. More intimately, we have the capacity to become what we see. We can take on something of the character of whatever we choose to focus on. This of course can be negative – there are plenty of dehumanizing, death-dealing images all around us – and we need to be aware, questioning and sometimes even resistant towards them, lest they shape the world and us in their damaging image.

But there is also the possibility of the image bringing good. True observation – attentive and loving observation – is not a dispassionate activity. If our attention is loving – not grasping but open to the otherness of the being or the object being seen – that person or object may mediate something sacred to us, and we may mediate something sacred to them. So the practice of *Choose Your Icons (Become What You See)* helps us to become aware of the images that shape us all, and offers the possibility of engaging with icons that may bring particular good to us and to the world around us.

Living with Icons

In the Jesus tradition the *meditation* (attention to) and the *mediation* (sharing) of the sacred take specific shape in the icons of the Orthodox churches. My own personal experience, learning from the Orthodox, is that icons are *lived with* rather than just *prayed with*. I pray with them, but they are more than mere aids into prayer. They are mothers and fathers, sisters and brothers, companions and friends. Icons are scattered around our house – on walls, on shelves, on window sills, on tables, by the bed. As I write this now I can see icons of Jesus Pantocrator (the risen Christ sustaining the cosmos) and a Mother and Child icon (a tender image of Mary and the infant Jesus). On the wall behind me is an icon

141

of the Holy Trinity (Andrei Rublev's much loved meditation on the life of the community of God). I don't have a dedicated icon-corner in the house at the moment (a Russian Orthodox practice) but I have done so in the past and that too has been helpful. When the time comes for focused prayer my practice is to light a candle, kiss the icon and sit with it. The icon begins to shift my attention from myself, from my stuff, from my small world to the possibility of the divine life that permeates and sustains everything. When my attention wanders (as it of course does) I come back to the icon, a visual stilling word.[2]

Icons are written (the word used to describe their careful process of creation) with great care, dedication and love, in a context of prayer. Icons are not worshipped. They do something altogether more interesting! They open up windows, doors or pathways onto the divine. They suggest a greater reality. And so they open us up, calling us out of our tendency to focus on ourselves, nudging us to remember our connectedness to the earth, to the people around us, and to God and the community of saints and angels. And like all sacred spaces, the icon is a gift that reminds us that the sacred is to be seen and encountered everywhere. See the Christ in the icon, and you may just begin to see the Christ in the face of the people you meet today, in the street, at work, in the store and in the café.

Choose Your Icons (Become What You See): A Practice

 Your icons are all around you. On your screens, on your walls, and in your magazines. This practice is about being intentional about the images we live with, and becoming the good thing that we see. So reflect on the images that you choose (or allow) to be your icon-companions. What's the wallpaper on your mobile, the screensaver on your desktop, the cover picture for your social

---

2 See Practice 8, 'Slow into Stillness' for more on the practice of the stilling word.

142

media, the picture stuck to your fridge, or the artwork on your wall? You can choose what you see and what you project. How is the hopeful nature of existence being expressed in the images you live with? Now seek out an image that seems to reflect what you value, and which might bring good to the world around you. Find ways to live with it for a week. Be aware of what the picture does to you. Let it shape your action to bring good to the world around you.

A step deeper into this tradition is to seek out an icon from the ancient Jesus tradition to accompany you in your stillness or prayer space. If you decide to do this, let the process be a prayerful one. May the icon that you need find you.

30

Stay in Your Spirit

SYMPHONY NO. 8
(WHAT WERE YOU THINKING?)

What were you thinking?
Were the doubts too strong,
the fear that eight would never be
seven or five, or two or three?

Did you consign the score to the flames
in one urgent movement, ashamed
or fearful you might thrust your hands
back in to love the piece again?
Or did you patiently turn each page into the fire
slowly building your theme – for some Norse god
the making of a funeral pyre?

Did the fire take hungrily,
the flames reclaim their own?
Or was the stove reluctant, holding back,
urging you to think again
refusing even in the end
to consume the ash
of your Aurora dream?

And in the cold next day
did you scoop the fragments from the grate
and begin to lay out a few, too late

and hear the spaces filled between
with hope of one more Northern spring?
What were you thinking?

(The Finnish composer Jean Sibelius is believed to have burned the manu-
script of what would have been his final symphony (no. 8) in 1945.)

*Andrew brought Simon to Jesus, who looked at him and said,
'You are Simon son of John. You are to be called Cephas' (which is
translated Peter).*

From the life of Jesus: John 1.42

The Spirit of St James' Park

Midway through the 2011–12 football season the famous English
club Newcastle United announced that St James' Park, iconic
home of the club since 1892, would be renamed using the name
of a company started up by the club owner, as a first step towards
licensing the full naming rights to the stadium in order to gener-
ate additional commercial revenue from advertising and sponsor-
ship. As the St James' Park name-plates came down opposition to
the change was immediate and widespread, far beyond the area
and across the world of football. Some supporters were charged
with criminal damage for painting the stadium's old name on its
walls. It appears that something deep in the club's great tradition
around respect for the history of the team, its relationship with
the supporters and its connection to the city had been discarded.
The *spirit of the club* had been ignored. Love and respect for the
name St James' Park expressed a spirit common to football fans
across the world – that football is primarily about the beautiful
game itself, about the people who play it and watch it, their places
and their stories – not about making money.

Your spirit is what people encounter when they meet you. It's
not about your achievements, nor is it about any of your perceived

failures. It's *how you are* as a human being. And *how you are* can change the world as much as anything you achieve. It may not be easy to identify your spirit. It's so close to us that we can find it hard to recognize. As with the St James' Park episode, we may only know what it is when it's broken. For almost six years I was part of mayBe, an experimental Anglican community in Oxford. One of the most important things we ever did (although we didn't know it at the time) was to try to understand our spirit – what it might be like (we hoped) to encounter this community. In the end seven words surfaced: grace : space : wonder : grit : resistance : laughter : presence.[1] Those words aren't a definitive take on what a community's spirit should be. And they aren't what *your* spirit should be. They are just the spirit of one community. But perhaps some elements within them might be shared by you and by your community, your project, your business or your work place.

Daisy Darling

In the same way that a community has a spirit, so has each individual human person. A key element of the task of becoming fully human is learning to stay in our spirit. There will always be pressures both internal and external trying to pull us away. Sooner or later our commitment to remaining in our spirit will be challenged. Here's a stanza from Karine Polwart's beautiful song 'Daisy (There are People)':

Hey Daisy darling don't spread your arms so wide
Why don't you keep a little something inside?
I know you think that hands are made for pulling us through
But there are people in this world who don't think like you
      do . . .[2]

---

1 'The spirit of mayBe' – www.maybe.org.uk.
2 'Daisy (There are People)' from *Scribbled in Chalk* by Karine Polwart, Hegri Music, 2006.

The young Daisy of the song has a spirit of openness, of trust in the other, and of willingness to help and be helped. But this may spirit not be shared – 'there are people in this world who don't think like you do'. We need to be prepared for the fact that some people won't share our spirit, and in tough truth some will be resistant to any sense of spirit that wants to bring good to the world. Don't let this deflect you from whatever you know is good and right.

But perhaps an even worse scenario is one in which we ourselves might be pushed – perhaps through fear, out of desperation or from weariness – to break our own spirit. Coming to understand and know our spirit, and then committing to it, will help us face this challenge. I don't have a tattoo. But if I did (and, heh, it's not too late), I'd make sure it was something that truly expressed my spirit.

Spirit Lost, Spirit Recovered

In the Gospels' lives of Jesus we discover a teacher who is adept at helping people to discover, live and stay in their spirit. His calling of potential disciples is not just about their following of him and his way. Rather, it's in their taking this path that they may live out who *they* truly are by discovering their calling[3] and their spirit. We see this in the story of the calling of the disciple we know as Peter. Originally named Simon, he receives a new name from Jesus – Cephas (in English, Peter). The root of this name means something like 'Rock'. Jesus recognizes the solid and dependable spirit of this man, and calls him to live out what is already there within him.

The irony, of course, is that when Jesus is arrested and his execution seems likely, this disciple Cephas, out of fear for his safety, breaks his own spirit of solidity by denying that he ever knew him. The tragedy of the rock-man breaking his own spirit

---

3 See Practice 24, 'Find Your Deep Flow'.

unfolds in front of us. But it's not the end of his story. What becomes beautifully apparent is that in the company of this Christ even the breaking of our own spirit is not the final word. The spirit can be recovered, even from a loss like this. And the resurrected Jesus brings Cephas to a resurrection of his spirit in a wonderful story of a shared breakfast on a beach in Galilee.[4] So if you have a broken spirit, or have even broken your own spirit, you are in good company, and in good hands. You may live in your spirit again.

Stay in Your Spirit: A Practice

 An important first step into the practice of *Stay in Your Spirit* is to try to understand what your spirit might be. Remember, this is *how you are*, and *what people encounter* when they meet you. So ask yourself, what do people encounter when they spend time with me? And what would I *wish* people to encounter when they meet me? Your spirit will reflect how you are at your best in reality and in aspiration. A good way into discovering, naming and living in our spirit is to experiment with writing, drawing, painting or making music for your spirit. What words come to mind? What shapes? What colours or sounds? And perhaps more adventurously, what might your spirit tattoo look like?

---

4 John 21 – see Practice 6, 'Kitchen Jazz'.

31

Dance Hands Open

A LOVE POEM FOR THE MAN

If on Fore Street today
I were to see you
would I find the courage
to seek my healing?
you do not know what you are asking for
to stretch out my arm?
what do you want me to do for you?
to touch your sleeve?
who touched me?
or to reach out and hold you?
do not hold on to me

So for now
on each in-breath
I will say your name
and on each out-breath
I will breathe your peace.
And this may be enough.

'*Truly I tell you, it will be hard for a rich person to enter the king-dom of heaven.*'

A teaching of Jesus: Matthew 19.23

Ducati 916

I'm in my middle age and still have never owned a Ducati 916. Nor a Triumph Bonneville T100. Nor a Harley Davidson Knucklehead. Nor indeed, any other motorbike. I say this with no pride. I wish I had one, gleaming outside the house right now. Never say never. It might still be a possibility, and there's nothing wrong with that. But, how easily we are transfixed by the things we desire or own! One of the great wisdom teachings of Buddhism is the need for us to detach ourselves from the things that hold us. Jesus echoes this learning. He understands the irony of ownership, the way we can become owned by the thing that we own. Ownership is power, but not always quite as we might have imagined it.

I'm calling this stance *Dance Hands Open*. Dancing through life with open hands means learning to carry lightly whatever we possess or care for. Our responsibilities and possessions are gifts, not our identity, nor our reason for being. Dancing with open hands keeps us humbly open to receiving the generosity of others, to receiving the benevolence of a cosmos pregnant with divine gift. Dancing with open hands also keeps us reaching out towards others. The things that come our way as possessions become gifts to be enjoyed, shared and passed on. Dancing with open hands ensures that we are open to joy.[1]

Hands Closed

There's a dancing-with-hands-open story in the Gospels in which a young man comes to Jesus and tells him that he wants to become one of his followers.[2] Jesus tells the man to sell all that he has, to give the money to the poor, and then follow him. The young man is saddened, we are told, because he is rich, and he goes away

---

1 For more musing on joy see Practice 28, 'Live from Your Joy'.

2 The story is told with their own emphases by three of the Gospel writers: Matthew 19.16–30, Mark 10.17–31 and Luke 18.18–30.

unable to fulfil his desire to follow this extraordinary rabbi. Jesus seems to understand what the potential points of compromise might be for each individual who comes to him. For the young man it's around his wealth. For another it might be around pride in their own goodness (check out his story of the Pharisee and the Tax Collector praying in the Temple[3]) or lack of action on behalf of those in trouble (see his famous story of the Priest, the Levite and Good Samaritan[4]).Each of these stories is in its own way also about living with or without hands open. The praying Pharisee's hands were closed around his own reputation. The hands of the travelling Priest and the Levite were closed around their own security on the road.

When we give it our attention, the scope of open-handedness begins to spread more widely. Our reputations, security, achievements, knowledge, skills and gifts are also best held lightly. As we get older the practice of open hands may come to be particularly important. If you've played and loved any team sport you'll know something of the feeling of loss that comes when you realize that you can't play at the same level as you once did. That moment came for me when I ran into a friend in a football game on the rec. Or did he run into me? Either way, he's a big boy, and it took me a while to get up. Time perhaps to take up another sport! A stance of dancing with open hands means that we may be better equipped to let go of a particular joy – and be ready to receive something new for the next season of life.

Dance and the Dancer

Whatever we 'own', it's important – and freeing – to see ourselves merely as grateful custodians or stewards, and just for a season of life. As the ownership impulse is so strong within us it's really helpful that there are seasons set aside in the Jesus tradition when

3 Luke 18.9–14.
4 Luke 10.25–37.

we can take a look at the ways in which we hold onto whatever we think is ours. The preparation time of Advent, and the self-examination period of Lent, work particularly well in this way. Has my possession of something actually become a situation in which I am being owned, manipulated or changed for the worse?

So why the idea of dance as a motif? I'm not a dancer (though I would love to have been). But I can shuffle, I can sway, I can even bob up and down. However you do it, there's something incredibly freeing about dancing. It requires us to (literally) step out of our normal mode of standing and walking and to move in a different way. At its best – imagine seeing a gifted group of contemporary dancers here – dancing is full of grace, expression and possibility. It's as if our hidden selves are being brought into the light and transformed. The dance and the dancer are entering into a greater flow that was always there but perhaps something we missed. This flow propels the dance, shapes it and pushes the dancer to do what he or she might never have envisaged or imagined. There's an energizing sense of momentum, with the dance and the dancer moving in an exchange of possibility. And of course dance usually requires the dancer to carry little in the way of props. The dance is life stripped back to its essence.

Dance Hands Open: A Practice

 If we see ourselves as dancing through life everything may begin to look a little different. It becomes full of possibility, provisionality, and light. Despite the famous hymn by Sydney Carter,[5] there seems to be no evidence that the rabbi Jesus could be found down at the dance hall in Nazareth. But it's clear that he lived a life of momentum, grace and purpose – with open hands to all that he encountered. His was a life in the spirit of dance. One of

---

5 'The Lord of the Dance'.

the reasons that he upset so many people was that he danced around and through some of the conventions, suppositions and power games of the day. Dance is, at its best, both joyful and subversive. It offers an alternative vision of the world. So in the spirit of the great teacher, let's dance!

Here's a tangible way into the practice of *Dance with Hands Open*. Find somewhere to dance. Big open spaces work as well as anything for this. And if this needs to be on your own that's fine. Turn your music to loud. And discover how natural – and good – it is to dance with hands open.

32

Less as More

GOING BACK TO PAPER

I'm going back to paper
and the snug fit of Heaney's pen.
The hard drive is fucked
wrote the man on his pad
your data is lost he said.
So I'm going back
to the open spaces of A3
to the mysterious flow of ink
and the splintering of graphite
into unexplored territory
full of possibility
onto a landscape
waiting for my commitment
to adventure
to beginning
just a line
a word
a letter
a stroke
a .

*Whoever does not receive the kingdom of God as a little child will
never enter it.*

A teaching of Jesus: Mark 10.15

Good Complication, Bad Complication

There are over 18,000 components in the latest Rolls Royce aero engine. We seem to have an inbuilt natural drift towards complication. A certain amount of complication is good, of course. The performance and reliability of the Rolls Royce Trent 1000 requires a certain level of skilled complication, for which passengers on any Boeing 787 will be grateful.

But this leaning towards complication in other areas can cause us to lose our balance. I've worked with organizations with a very clear sense of what they are about. I've also encountered organizations that bury themselves in piles of ever-increasing levels of strategy and tactics. Papers follow papers following papers. Meetings produce meetings producing meetings. Once the process has begun it seems to build a momentum of its own. Complication can lead us to miss the point of what we are about! Perhaps more importantly, in a wider context, the future flourishing of the human race and the planet will depend to a great extent on a new commitment to simplicity.

The Myth of Perpetual Economic Growth

Today the FTSE 100 is down 2.44. The Dow Jones is up 3.70. The Nikkei is down 14.55. Perpetual economic growth as a model, a goal or even a necessity seems to be widely accepted in the current political landscape. I believe that this faith in perpetual growth is misguided, damaging and even pernicious. While our economies continue to grow, the need to share our resources more equally can be conveniently discarded in favour of some concept of wealth 'trickling down'. Now, if the planet, if each continent, if each city had unlimited resources the idea of trickle-down might just make some sense. But of course our resources are limited. We can't grow for ever. The idea of perpetual growth is bad for our neighbour, bad for the earth, and bad for us. We need to find another way, another creed, another goal. I want to suggest that this needs to be the pursuit, not of perpetual growth, but of perpetual *harmony*, perpetual *partnership*, perpetual *simplicity*.

As indicated by all the practices in *Running Over Rocks*, any change for good in the wider world needs to begin with us. So this stance of *Less as More* is about seeking harmony, partnership and simplification in our relationship with the earth and with each other. It's about abandoning our false complexities and discovering a new simplicity.

Learning from a Child

Jesus teaches the importance of moving away from a false idea of maturity – a power-oriented way of living in which we force ourselves upon the world – towards a new maturity in which we learn to live with, alongside and in partnership with all that exists, like a child opening up to a new experience with love and grace. Please note the difference between simplicity and simplistic. Jesus is not suggesting a move backwards towards the simplistic (a naive, ignorant or foolish outlook) but an enlightened movement into the simplicity of a life lived in loving engagement with the world to which we belong.

In the Gospel of Matthew the writer shows[1] how Jesus deals with a problematic kind of complication in his context – complication in religious practice, with many rites, roles and reputations dependent upon ever more elaborate application of rules and definitions. Jesus is asked a question intended to catch him out, by revealing his lack of commitment to the detail of the law: 'Teacher, which commandment in the law is the greatest?'[2] Jesus' reply is a simple but powerful and harmonious summary of the law, cutting through all the complications and details that have

---

1 Matthew 22 and 23.
2 Matthew 22.37–40.

entwined themselves around it: *Love God. And love your neighbour as yourself.*

Another Measure: Happy Planet

So how might 'Love God and love your neighbour' shape a world in which the rolling TV news invariably closes with the supposed joy or gloom of a rising or falling stock market? Could there be another measure than economic growth? I like the work of the Happy Planet Index[3] created by Nic Marks, a project of the New Economics Foundation.[4] Using global data in a powerful equation (experienced well-being x life expectancy / ecological footprint) it's perhaps no surprise that the countries that emerge as happiest are parts of the world where life seems to be encountered with greater simplicity.[5] Not everyone agrees, of course (check out the tweets), but I find the index to be persuasive.

One of the most striking conclusions of the Happy Planet Index is that no single country is revealed to be 'good' in all three areas. At the same time it's hopeful to note that no country is classed as 'poor' in all three. It feels fanciful to imagine that the TV news might one day replace its obsessive tracking of the FTSE 100, Dow Jones and Nikkei with an update from the Happy Planet Index – but why not! A growing economy may not be the only measure of a good life. In fact, it may be a sign of a truly mature society when it begins to treat economic growth in a much more nuanced way and ask questions like: To what extent does this growth make possible sustainable happiness here? In what ways does this growth contribute to the happiness of our neighbours? How can this growth enhance the well-being of the planet? And what might replace the goal of perpetual economic growth as a policy in our context?

3 www.happyplanetindex.org.
4 www.neweconomics.org.
5 Happiest five in 2012: Costa Rica, Vietnam, Colombia, Belize, El Salvador.

Less as More: A Practice

I'm calling this stance of harmony, partnership and simplicity *Less as More*. It must begin where we are, in everyday actions, and it can look something like this. Wherever and whenever you have a choice to make today, consider the more simple solution as a possible option. Whether you are choosing clothes to wear for work, a sandwich to buy for lunch, or a colour to paint a wall, a choice towards harmony and simplicity is possible. You won't always choose the simpler option – sometimes there will be other considerations that hold sway – but the act of making the simple option a genuine possibility may encourage us to keep locating ourselves on that more harmonious path – towards a more serene way of life that helps shape a truly happy planet.

33

Everything as Extraordinary

JESUS PLAYS FOR BARCELONA

We waited years for one to appear
but finally this poet came near
and his beautiful lines took our breath away
a blur of red and blue on green, a play-
maker threading all our desires
into such exquisite spaces
dancing close and through and around
in a whir of light and colour and sound
an epic poem that left us
silent and shouting for more. Jesus
plays for Barcelona!

*Blessed are you, Lord God of all creation, for through your
goodness we have received the bread we offer you: fruit of the earth
and work of human hands, it will become for us the bread of life.*

Words from the Mass, Roman Missal, third edition, 2012

Red and Blue on Green

Lionel Messi's sublime goal on 54 minutes was just one peak
moment in many. Watching TV coverage of FC Barcelona winning
the 2011 Champions League Final – an experience of beauty that

rivalled anything I had recently come across in any area of human (or any other) activity – kick-started the process that led to the poem 'Jesus plays for Barcelona'. That late-May night at Wembley stadium, Barcelona's flowing passing game, a multi-paced blur of red and blue on green, was a truly wondrous thing.

Once you begin to see beauty *somewhere*, you begin to see that beauty really is just about *everywhere*. It's close at hand, a glance away, even under our feet. I rather like metal drain covers. Surprisingly perhaps, there are some beautiful drain covers, and more than you might imagine. They don't need to be beautiful, of course, they just need to be effective. To be strong enough to protect the drain from us and us from the drain. So when I come across a beautiful cover in the street, I'll take a picture and wonder at the process that brought it into being. Why did someone bother to make this most mundane of objects so visually pleasing?

In the street where we used to live in Oxford there is a series of covers made by the Broads Manufacturing Company of Paddington London. The edge of the cover is all curves, a circle with three smaller circles at 12 o'clock, 4 and 8 (or north, south-east and south-west). In my imagination it looks like the outline of Rupert Bear's head from the classic cartoon. The grips on the cover's face are small raised squares, each on a slightly different trajectory, oriented towards the centre point. Late afternoon or early morning are the best times to see these industrial wonders, as the increasing slant of the light lifts the grips, casts long shadows, and brings out the metal's own reds and blues.

Letting in the Light

Earlier I suggested the importance of seeing the sacred beauty of the earth and its creatures.[1] In the next series of practices there's one focused on seeing the amazing light in each other.[2] But to

---

1 See Practice 2, 'Walk the Good Earth', and Practice 3, 'Close-up (Terra Divina)'.
2 See Practice 37, '*Namaste* (I See the Light in You!)'.

bring good to the world around us we also need to learn to see the beauty of human activity already present in the world. This practice is about beginning to see the extraordinary nature of – well – almost everything!

It's easy to become cynical about humanity, to see the worst. And you don't have to go far to find it. The apparent worst is all around us if we look for it. But that worst is not the whole picture. Our best refuses to let go. Often this best is quieter, less obvious, but it's there waiting for us all the same. So the practice of *Everything as Extraordinary* is a commitment to wonder at the brilliance of human endeavour and ingenuity. It's also a recognition that beauty can change us for good. Much of what we human beings create, make and produce is truly amazing. Just today I've enjoyed seeing the curve of a railway line; hearing the hum of a chainsaw; working with the possibility of an iPad.

Almost everything is extraordinary, but it would be hard to live just a day if our senses were permanently tuned in to the true nature of everything. Perhaps we negotiate life by letting much of its beauty remain hidden, under the surface, a little out of reach. We would surely be dazzled if we could see the true depth of the beauty of the world, the deep wonder of our fellow human beings, and the amazing grace of their best actions. But long before we risk being dazzled, the first challenge for most of us is to begin to let the light in. It's vital to nurture our sense of the beauty that *can* be endured, our sense of what *can* be gazed upon.

Staring Out of the Window

You can see beauty everywhere. But to see *Everything as Extraordinary* takes time. It requires our attention. This is the arena of the great nature poets and artists. It's also the field of the best scientists and engineers, cooks and journalists, mechanics and hairdressers, footballers and teachers. Actually, to be truly responsive and creative in *any* area of human activity a willingness to give deep attention is required. Attention is the groundwork of all who are in thrall to the wonder of existence, not seeing just what we expect to see, but open to being surprised. However, to allow our attention to be caught is not always treated as a positive thing. Staring out of the window wasn't well received at the schools I attended! But staring out of the window, and allowing our attention to be caught, might be just what is required if we are to see what is truly going on.

I'll say more about the Eucharist[3] – perhaps the central practice of the Jesus tradition, emerging from the great Jewish meal of salvation, the Passover – later in *Running Over Rocks*, but here I just want to point out its often neglected but vital and ancient role in the celebration of beauty: more particularly, for celebrating the beauty of God's paradise, both now and in whatever is to come, and celebrating our participation in it. The making of bread and the production of wine are astonishing events, beautiful collaborations of the giftedness of earth, human endeavour and the community of God. And if we learn to see the beauty in the act of bread-making ('fruit of the earth and work of human hands') and wine-growing ('fruit of the vine and work of human hands')[4] we may just begin to see the beauty everywhere.

Everything as Extraordinary: A Practice

 Wherever you go today, take a camera or cameraphone with you. Take pictures whenever your attention is caught by beauty, particularly by earthy human interventions in the landscape – like pavements and grilles, posters and signs, glass and walls. Enjoy the extraordinary beauty that you find. Allow yourself to be drawn into a landscape that is often ignored. Sense

---

3 See Practice 43, 'Eucharist (Taste Paradise)'.
4 Roman Missal, third edition, 2012.

your own participation in a paradise hidden in plain view. If you want further inspiration check out the brilliant close-observation work of photographer-artist Steve Broadway, in which he takes a daily look at the world around him.[5] And so begin to see that everything is extraordinary.

---

5 www.onedaylikethistoday.blogspot.co.uk.

34

Fight Dragons, with Humility

NOTHING TO SAY

The more I find my voice
the less I know
and the less, I know
there is to say.

The more reason
to kneel hands open
in silence –
to attend the Teacher's flowers of the field
to be in the wonder of it all
and to get out of the way.

The more I find my voice
the less I know
and the less, I know
there is to say.

Blessed are the poor in spirit, for theirs is the kingdom of heaven.

A teaching of Jesus: Matthew 5.3

Here be Dragons

HIC SVNT DRACONES. There's a long-established tradition in map-making of marking the map's unknown edges with references to the dangers that lurk there, just out of sight. The Hunt-Lenox Globe – an extraordinary model of the earth, only five inches in diameter, fashioned around 1510 and now in the New York Public Library – carries the marking HIC SVNT DRACONES, Latin for 'here be dragons', in the sea off the coasts of East Asia. We might wish that there be no dragons here, there or anywhere. But in life, dragons of all sorts there are. So what kind of personal stance could help us to negotiate the areas of our life-maps where dragons appear? Sometimes, of course, only courage will see off the dragons and see us through.[1] But this stance offers a complementary, and perhaps surprising, possibility as we seek to find a way to look up and face the dragons that step into our path.

We are conditioned, it seems, to imagine that our position (whatever position we are in) is always under some kind of threat. The fear of dragons both describes and fuels this experience. This sense of threat may have its roots in our age-old learning how to survive as early humans. So to break out of this way of thinking will take determination. Some wariness of danger is obviously helpful. That sometimes *here and there be dragons* that may cause us harm, usually these days in some form of dehumanizing human activity, is not in doubt. But the presence and the danger of dragons can be exaggerated. The dragons we fear may not be so many, and may not be so threatening as we imagine.

Overcoming Guns with Flowers

Nevertheless sometimes, here and there, be dragons. So what is to be done? How can we resist them? Returning fire with fire may occasionally have its place, but the fire of dragons is often best not

---

1 See Practice 41, 'Choose Courageous'.

fought with fire. I want to suggest the possibility of humility as a stance with which to engage the dragons we face. The necessity for humility was a constant theme in the learning of those earliest monastics, the Desert Fathers and Mothers. How can we overcome our demons? asked Amma Theodora. Only through humility. This is interesting, because it feels almost like the opposite of what we should do. But it rings true in the best of human experience.

Some of the most momentous moments in the human story have come when people have discovered the strength of humility in resistance. So in the spring of 1930 Mahatma Gandhi leads the Salt March adopting his principle of Satyagraha – 'asking for truth' without violence – in a protest against British rule in India. In October 1967 17-year-old Jane Rose Kasmir holds a daisy up to the rifle barrels and bayonets of the National Guard during an anti-Vietnam War protest[2] outside the Pentagon in Washington DC. On 5 June 1989 in Tiananmen Square in Beijing an unknown man with shopping bags stands in front of a column of tanks, repeatedly moving into their path. This is humility overcoming dragons, demons and all kinds of dehumanizing force.

Blessed are the Poor in Spirit

Usually, thankfully, the dragons that most of us face will be less powerful and more ordinary than soldiers, tanks and guns. But we still need to work out how to face them. The sense of being excluded by others, for example, can be just as powerful in later life as it was in the school playground. If we begin to accept our exclusions with humility, something interesting happens. The pain of the exclusion begins to fade, and the world which seemed so centred in that excluding place begins to reveal itself as much bigger, much wider, much more graceful. And rather than feeling anger towards those who exclude us, we may even begin to find

---

2 A famous image by French photo-journalist Marc Riboud.

ourselves able to practise compassion towards them. Their exclusion of others is after all usually just coming from their own fear of dragons, a fear that we share.

As Matthew arranges it, pride of place in the listing of the Beatitudes – the core sayings of Jesus – goes to his teaching on humility. 'Blessed are the poor in spirit, for theirs is the kingdom of heaven.' This takes Jesus' teaching in a radically different direction from much of what has gone before, and from most of what is yet to come. Being poor in spirit is about grounding ourselves in the freeing truths that *we are loved and we belong*. Being poor in spirit is about shaping a life of strength from humility – a strength that Jesus teaches will enable us to both 'move mountains'[3] and face our own internal dragons or 'demons'. We may learn that we are not at the centre of everything, neither is my dragon or your dragon the most fearful, the most unusual or most interesting of dragons. It's just another dragon. Encountering dragons is just part of every human story. And we may discover too the wisdom not to identify ourselves with our dragons. Your dragon is not you!

Fight Dragons, with Humility: A Practice

So how do we practise humility? *Fight Dragons, with Humility* is a stance, a way of being that we need to learn and to which we commit ourselves until it becomes once again a natural element of our being. But there are some physical actions that we can take to help us find this path and keep on it. A gesture of humility when we meet people can be really important. You'll need to find your own, but it will be the opposite of the many gestures of power that people make all the time with or without knowing it. A slight bowing of the head, with hands held together towards the lips, as if in prayer, is received as a gesture of humility across many

---

3 Matthew 17.20.

cultures and traditions. And the simple act of stepping aside on the pavement to let someone pass or in a doorway to let someone go first can be full of surprise and giftedness. Look for a gesture of humility that sits well in your own skin and in your setting, and that communicates how you are attempting to live. It may also be a physical reminder to you in your own body of the path you are taking to freedom. Here and there be dragons. But they will always be overcome by the strength of humility.

35

Love Your Place

NIGHT JAZZ AT CLAPHAM JUNCTION

The city squats
down
for the minutes between late and early
catching its breath, settling into the night's doorway
under a blanket of discarded stories.

Sodium lights up the sky
wondering what might come into being
in this brief edge time
of noisy silence.

A night train clatters its rhythm
a generator hums a bass line
a siren trumpet-kicks into a melody
and a conversation on the 16th floor
becomes the vocal improvising
night jazz at Clapham Junction.

Blessed are the meek, for they will inherit the earth.

A teaching of Jesus: Matthew 5.5

Where are You From?

I'm not sure where I'm from. But I do know where I *am*. The concept of being *from somewhere* is complicated if you have lived in lots of places and been shaped in some way by them all. There is a giftedness in knowing where you are from. People with a strong family connection to a particular village, valley, town or city quarter may be fortunate, particularly if the connection goes back centuries. But for many of us now this is less and less usual. The poem 'Night jazz at Clapham Junction' came out of a visit to a friend whose flat looks out over Clapham Junction towards the centre of London. This place is so different from where I live. I found myself entranced by the night-time sight and soundscape. What, I find myself asking, might it be like to belong here?

This stance is about nurturing a sense of belonging *wherever* we are, believing that this will be good for us and good for those around us. There will be some links here to the earlier chapter on loving our roots[1] – but this practice is strongly focused on our connection to the place in which we find ourselves *now*, rooting ourselves here. This can transform the way that we feel about a place. And perhaps more importantly it can change how we bring good to a place and to its people.

Every Place a Thin Place

I have experienced the inspirational reality of what have memorably been called 'thin places', those spaces and moments where any perceived gap between the earthy and the spiritual seems to shrink. Here what usually seems like a solid and impenetrable barrier can give way to a flexing porous skin. It's as if the shape, movement and texture of the sacred can be almost discerned. So, while alone in a medieval church I have sensed being surrounded by those who had been there before. In contemplation with an icon

---

1 See Practice 13, 'Love Your Roots'.

I've encountered a hint of Mother Julian's discovery of the radical OK-ness of everything (all will be well). And in an open field that felt like a cathedral I've sensed an embracing personal presence in the Eucharist. These are thin places. But they are gifts to remind us that the mystery, the sacred, the God is everywhere. And is actually to be encountered in the ordinary, in the everyday, wherever we find ourselves. Every place is a thin place. Even the most unpromising place is full of possibility. And deserves our love.

One of the brilliant awkwardnesses of the ancient Jesus tradition is that this revelation of the nature of the community of God – the life of the man Jesus – took place in a small, localized place at a certain moment of time. The cosmic Christ (gift for all peoples, for all times, for all places) is encountered in a particular man (Yeshua/Jesus) in a particular place (Nazareth) at a particular fleeting moment (what we call the first century AD). This is both the great puzzle and the great gift of the Incarnation – God come among us. And it's part of the background to one of Jesus' core sayings: 'Blessed are the meek, for they shall inherit the earth.' The brilliant, the far-reaching, the world-changing things we hope for (the inheriting of the earth) can only take shape in the unspectacular settings of the everyday and the everyplace (in the being meek). I really enjoy collaborating with the artist and illustrator Si Smith. In one project we've done together the resurrection of Jesus is set in Si's home city of Leeds in the north of England. To see through Si's brilliant images the great story set in the streets, parks and pubs of the city is to recognize the sacredness of this – and every – place.[2]

Brunel's Bridge

I love the interconnectedness of the world. Every day I'm working and communicating with people around the globe via the internet and social media. There's great energy, synergy and learning in

---

2 www.proost.co.uk/stations-resurrection, www.simonsmithillustrator.co.uk.

this daily exchange. It's amazing to sense that I belong to networks across the planet. But there's also a place for local belonging.

I love living in south Devon. I write a lot about the joy of finding my place in the rural landscape here. But I'm also getting to know and love our closest city. Some people dislike Plymouth, and the rebuilding of the city centre after it was bombed in the Second World War is not to everyone's taste. But there's something about the spirit of this city by the sea, with its back to the high and wild Dartmoor, linked to our neighbours in Cornwall by Brunel's distinctive 1859 Royal Albert rail bridge and its 1960s roadway companion. I love the history of this place, its connections to the defence of Britain and its place in the birth-story of the United States of America. I like the art of Robert Lenkiewicz. I rather like a lot of the architecture. And I'm rooting for the city's football and rugby union teams to recover. I'm not trying to sell this city to you. The point is that it is our local city, and I want to connect with it, to love it, to be part of it.

Love Your Place: A Practice

 The practice of *Love Your Place* starts with our home and work spaces. This is not about creating a perfect home or an impressive work-station, but about creating a space that reflects what really matters to you. If the space does this it will energize you for the life you lead. It will also be a gift to those who encounter you there. So a question – to what extent does your home or work space reflect whatever you feel you are truly 'about'? Does this place feel loved?

Then moving your attention out into your locality or neighbourhood, consider how you feel about this place. Ask yourself these questions and see what action they may lead you into: What draws you to this place? What do you find difficult? How could you express your belonging here? And how could you love this place more?

PRACTICES OF PEACE

From despondency towards transformation:
bringing good to the world

It had been cold, wet and overcast for weeks in South Devon. Then one winter afternoon the sky began to clear. I returned to the edge-space of the shore, looking for light, again.

In this series of practices we move further into possibilities of bringing good to the world. Our own learning to run over rocks is not just a personal mission of discovery – although it must begin there. Our ability to spring from boulder to boulder must be a gift for others. We need to move from despondency towards transformation, from despair or inertia at the way things are towards something much more hopeful, bringing good to the world. And the thread that runs through all these practices is the possibility that through them we might bring peace. Peace in the world takes shape through us discovering our own peace.

The season connected with these Practices of Peace is Trinity and its stunning high-point the Transfiguration. In the season of Trinity the divine is perceived as a community of persons, a community of

173

love bringing love. This Holy Trinity of God invites us to enter into the divine life, to discover it in the world and to allow it to transform us so that we might enable further transformation towards a more peaceable world. In the festival of the Transfiguration (a revelation of transformation) the tradition glimpses how everything, despite appearances, is becoming peaceful and peaceable. The man Jesus is momentarily seen shining with light, his true divinity revealed. At the same time, the sacred nature of the world is revealed, our own becoming divine is glimpsed, and our calling to help reshape the world towards peace is given new impetus and meaning. The peace we seek for the world is already within us.

36

Re-imagine the World

YOU TAGGED ME

One night you came to our street
with your spray cans and tape,
your mask, and a heart
full of beautiful ideas, bold marks
from your ragged dreams.
And you tagged me.

So it seems
my head is now full
of flowers and faces, of
stars and traces of light
breaking down walls
cutting into canals
shining under bridges –
the rough but bright edges
of a new earth coming into being.

One night you came to our street
with your spray cans and tape,
your mask, and a heart
full of beautiful ideas, bold marks
from your ragged dreams.
And you tagged me.
And my tired dreams are remade.

You are the salt of the earth; but if salt has lost its taste, how can its saltiness be restored?

A teaching of Jesus: Matthew 5.13

Another World is Possible!

The prophets are on the streets. And they are proclaiming that 'another world is possible'. This tagline of the Occupy London site at St Paul's Cathedral in 2011 would have been recognized by the prophets of the Jewish scriptures. The way things are is not the way things always need to be. There are other possibilities! And we can begin to change the world through our imaginations. Not imagining as pretending, but imagining as thinking, as believing, as yearning, as praying and as acting, bringing into being something new.

The river of re-imagining is fed by many streams. There may be our own disquiet at something that is going on right now. There's the wisdom of those who have re-imagined before us (of course others have done this work before!). And there are the insights of re-imagining taking shape in the various spiritual and religious traditions. In all this re-imagining it's important to be against what is wrong. But to a certain extent that is the easy part. The demanding thing is to work out what a true alternative might be, being ready to propose it, and then being willing get involved in the tough work of enabling it to happen. This requires vision and persistence, humility and strength, and a willingness to embody the solution in ourselves.

Like Salt

Jesus used a tasty metaphor from his own setting for this task of re-imagining the world. You must, he said, be like salt! You've got to bring flavour and sharpness to appetites that have lost the sense that change for good is possible, to appetites that all too easily settle for a bland diet of same-as-usual or for the junk food of the status quo. There's an important insight from the teacher's metaphor in that the salt isn't the main thing. The food to which the salt is added is the main thing; the salt provides the sharpness and the flavour, and preserves what is good. So re-imagining the world is not about us – that would be yet one more ego-trip. Our role is to bring out, encourage or enhance the capacity and impetus for change that is already present all around us.

I'm calling this practice of peace *Re-imagine the World*. So what is bothering you at this time? What do you sense could be your contribution here? There's an interesting element in a story from the life of Jesus that we mused on earlier,[1] which I think may reflect the importance of this question. In Matthew's telling of the story of the woman who anoints Jesus, the Disciples complain about the waste of this expensive fragrance. It could, they say, be used for the poor (and to re-imagine the world in that way). Jesus disagrees, 'for the poor you will always have with you'. He is suggesting that we can't all do everything all the time. But the important thing is that we are doing *something* to re-imagine the world, and perhaps crucially *doing the one thing* that we are somehow meant to do.

There's something important here about vocation or calling. You will almost certainly find yourself moved by particular issues or possibilities. This is a gift. Your own story may be interacting here with a wider story, an episode or experience in your life journey connecting with a wider issue. Before I was adopted my adoptive parents lost two sons very young. Among their many disabilities was blindness. Some years later my parents became involved with a charity that works with people with visual impairment. For the rest of their lives they have poured their experience, compassion and gifts into that work, re-imagining the world from the heart of their own story.

---

1 See Practice 1, 'Come Home to Your Body'.

From Protest to Party

A key element in the work of re-imagining the world is the need to hold both reality and hope. The way things are is the way things are. But things can and must and in many cases *will be* different. And *hopefulness* in the possibility of change for good is something that needs nurturing. I've been interested and inspired by a discovery of the Transition Network[2] (based near to me in Totnes): in their experience, any action people take to care for the earth is proving much more effective whenever that action is shared and practised in a hopeful way, when the emphasis is on 'daring to dream', and as a result when the action taken feels more like a party than a protest. Not only is global action best begun locally, it is best done, they suggest, in a spirit of hope, even of celebration.

Sometimes protest needs to happen.[3] Sometimes resistance needs to take place. But I sense that our re-imagining of the good world may almost always be more effective if the shaping of that re-imagining leans towards hope, towards possibility, even towards joy. Perhaps this may be a true test of the depth of our re-imagining. If our re-imagined world is actually just another joyless vision without soul and grace it will be little better than whatever it seeks to replace. The re-imagined world must be a place of both tears and laughter.

Re-imagine the World: A Practice

So how do we work out what we could or should be doing to *Re-imagine the World*? There may need to be an element of self-education here. We may need to engage with the media to understand the issues that are around. If you do that, don't rely on one source of news alone. Research the different views present

2 www.transitionnetwork.org.
3 See Practice 38, 'Speak up! Speak out!'

in the media, see what's getting covered (or missed) in social media, and if the issue has a local aspect try to engage with it on the ground where you are. Also take time to ponder on whatever your own story may be telling you. How might your life journey to this point have prepared you for a particular cause? What are you being called to do and to be as a joyful re-imaginer in tough times – bringing *flowers and faces, stars and traces of light* to your street? Let's *Re-imagine the World*!

37

Namaste
(I See the Light in You!)

HESITANT LIKE HORSES

Hesitant,
like horses
our heads together
brushing skin, breathing deep
eyes wide, senses seeking reassurance
to love and be loved.
All our times reflected in this instant:
the first glance of desiring that we shared
the last gaze of knowing that we will hold
this moment's glimpse of us as we are
hesitant before the wonder
of another. Hesitant,
like horses.

Blessed are the merciful, for they will receive mercy

A teaching of Jesus: Matthew 5.7

Full of Light

You are amazing. I know it's rude to stare, but it's hard to tear myself away. *Namaste (I See the Light in You!)*.[1] You are full of light. This practice of bringing peace is about seeing the wonder in another person. It's about recognizing their extraordinary being, and sensing that this is so mysterious and so good and so potentially peaceful that we might even say it's about coming to recognize the divine nature of every human being we meet.

To see the sacred in another person we must first learn to see the sacred in ourselves. The Orthodox followers of Jesus have a term for this. They call it theosis. This describes a process of stepping into our true nature as sacred beings united with the sacred we call God. It's an exercise in recognizing our own extraordinary nature. It may be challenging. On any given day we may feel far from extraordinary! So, like many of the practices in *Running Over Rocks*, the practice of *Namaste (I See the Light in You!)* will require us to learn to truly see what is going on. We'll need to step out of ourselves, to begin to see through all our mixed motives and through all our inconsistent actions, to begin to discern the glory of the human being that lies at our core.

I See You

To see the light in the other will sometimes be demanding. Most days we will come across someone whose damaging actions or damaged spirit will sorely test our belief that this particular human being is a wonder-filled creature. But even here there will almost always still be some small specks of the great light that enabled our coming into human-being. Our divine nature is there all the time, but can be submerged by the stuff that comes our way and by the stuff we accumulate, so we'll need to watch for it with great desire

---

1 *Namaste* – a greeting from the Indian subcontinent meaning something like 'I reverence you'.

and persistence, like whale-watchers scanning the ocean, hoping for that moment to come when a fin breaks the surface in a beautiful arc.

At the core of the goodness of the Na'vi, the sapient humanoid inhabitants of the moon Pandora in James Cameron's film *Avatar*, is their saying, 'I see you.' This phrase reflects their ability to see the wonder of the other, and it enables them to bring good to their world. Our equivalent of 'I see you' seeing must include being real about the dehumanizing process that the other may be exhibiting. This dark aspect of their journey must not be missed or glossed over. The tragedy of the less-than-human human being needs to be mourned. But this seeing will also mean that we may begin to see the wonder of the person, their possibility and their gift to the world, however far from realization that may seem.

This is Mercy

Jesus lived a life of 'I see you.' In the Gospels we find him continually recognizing the true worth of people who have been discarded, excluded, abused or forgotten. He sees the wholeness of people whom others see only as incomplete, imperfect or broken. One of Jesus' key teachings is about the way we see (and therefore treat) others: 'Blessed are the merciful, for they will receive mercy.' He might equally have said, 'Blessed are those who truly see others, for they will be truly seen.'

Mercy feels like an old-fashioned kind of word. But its time has never gone away. I'm not talking here about the kind of mercy that's part of a power game, where mercy is given or withheld according to the whim of the powerful. The mercy that I am talking about here reaches out beyond any concept of deserving or undeserving and beyond any sense of its belonging to the one giving it. True mercy is about acknowledging the wonder in the face of the other, however much that person may not know it, show it or practise it. It can therefore be a demanding thing to handle. But it may just be a crucial secret that enables a more peaceable world as envisaged by Jesus.

Namaste (I See the Light in You!): A Practice

 One way into the practice of Namaste *(I See the Light in You!)* is to nurture an awareness of how you are seeing others. Try to catch yourself whenever you are making an assumption about someone, and therefore potentially when you are judging them (another of Jesus' teachings focuses specifically on the damage caused by judging others). This can be alarming. You'll soon realize how frequently you are looking for the small darknesses in others, not seeing their greater light. But with persistence and practice you will find that by catching yourself you can stop that judging process, and exchange it for a seeing-with-mercy, embodying the love that is already moving towards the other.

A deeper step into this practice is to begin to use the Orthodox 'Jesus Prayer'. My experience of mercy has been deeply shaped in recent years by my engagement with this prayer: '*Lord Jesus Christ, Son of God, have mercy upon me, a sinner*.'[2] For a long time I'd struggled to use the prayer, with its seeming focus on our sinfulness. Two things began to change that. One was a gradual realization that God need no longer be feared, as I came to a sense that God is above all things relentless love. Check out how one of Jesus' youngest followers came to see God in the light of his experience of being with Jesus,[3] and the wisdom of the great Desert Father we know as Abba Anthony.[4]

The second was a conversation with a wise nun who told me that in the Jesus prayer sin is best understood as our tendency to

---

2 The Jesus Prayer in its classic long form.

3 See the disciple John's reflection discussed in Practices 44, 'Pilgrimage (On the Road)' and 48, 'Sacramental Life (Live the Brilliant Future Now)'.

4 'I no longer fear God, but I love him. For love casts out fear': Abba Anthony.

orient ourselves in the wrong direction. That made sense to me. Life is all about orientation and movement. So when we pray 'have mercy upon me, a sinner' we're acknowledging the love to which we are drawn, seeking help to keep on orienting ourselves this way, and asking for help to live a life of mercy towards others. So this is mercy: the beloved coming home to the love that is always moving towards the beloved. Let the wisdom of the *Namaste* practice shape the way that you see. And so again, the world will be reshaped just a little, for good . . .

38

Speak Up! Speak Out!

ONE HUNDRED MILLION SEEDS

The boy who played on a dirt cave floor
has been walled up.
The man who wove a bird's nest for the world
has been taken away.
The sower who sowed one hundred million seeds
has been concealed.
Without tools, far from sunlight, away from rain
in hard ground.

So they came for the gardener
in the end
as they always do:
too close to the earth
too familiar with buds
too conscious of spring.

But the dirt will sing out
and the flowers will bear witness
and one hundred million seeds will shout his name
Ai Weiwei!
Ai Weiwei!
Ai Weiwei!

(The artist Ai Weiwei created *Sunflower Seeds 2010* for an exhibition at Tate Modern.)

Blessed are those who hunger and thirst for righteousness, for they will be filled.

A teaching of Jesus: Matthew 5.6

Telling Truth to Power

'If we don't push, there's nothing happening.'
'I act brave because I know the danger is really there.'
'If you don't act the danger becomes stronger.'
'Once you've experienced [freedom], it remains in your heart.'[1]

Our part in creating a path to a more just world can and must begin here and now. It's time to *Speak Up! Speak Out!* It's time to tell the truth to power. And there have never been so many accessible ways to do this. The social media are changing the way that movements for justice can build momentum. The situation for which you seek justice may be five minutes' walk from your door. It may also be 5,000 miles away. It could be both. And you can be involved. It's at your fingertips.

The poem 'One hundred million seeds' began to form in the spring of 2011, when the Chinese artist Ai Weiwei was arrested by the authorities and removed from sight without charge or information. A poem on the internet was my small attempt to *Speak Up! Speak Out!* on an issue about which I felt strongly. On its own, of course, my poem made no difference at all. It was just one small action. But it was a tiny drop in a mighty ocean of protest from around the world. And the ocean made a difference. Ai Weiwei's detention did not go unnoticed (unlike so many of the disappeared). Truth was told to power. And in the end Ai Weiwei was released, albeit with restrictions on his freedom of movement, ever-stricter surveillance, and with hefty (and contested) charges of tax-avoidance.

---

1 Ai Weiwei in the 2012 film *Ai Weiwei: Never Sorry*, directed by Alison Klayman.

The Need to be Hungry and Thirsty

This practice of *Speak Up! Speak Out!* is about coming out and stepping up in our resistance to injustice. The practice is almost always a costly one. The dealers of injustice do not look kindly on those who stand up to them. As Jesus makes clear in another of his core-saying Beatitudes, righteousness will need to be hungered and thirsted for. It won't come easily. The righteousness we need to work for, wherever we are in the world, is a state in which everything good flourishes and everything destructive fades away. In his context Jesus described this as the 'kingdom of heaven'. Right now this state of peaceful and peaceable existence may seem very far off, but for Jesus this righteousness is a state of being that begins now – or it does not begin at all.[2]

One of the tough aspects of the calling to *Speak Up! Speak Out!* is to recognize that injustice in some form seems to be flourishing everywhere. So we need to work out how not to be overwhelmed by it, not beaten down by it, not embittered by it, and not changed by it. Otherwise we may find that in time we too may have become a source of injustice, justifying to ourselves any instinctive-but-vengeful response by suggesting that injustices' perpetrators 'had it coming'. So this practice is also about reaching beyond the understandable temptation to simply kick out at injustice (and how it really does need kicking, we say!) to offer a far better, peace-bringing possibility to the world around us.

Walk Humbly

This leads us to the demanding truth that justice has to live first within us. According to the ancient prophets of Judah–Israel, forerunners of the teacher-prophet Jesus, the great complaint of God was that the people who complained at the injustice of the nations around them had actually become a source of injustice themselves:

---

2 The theologian Paul Tillich speaks of resurrection in these terms.

'Your wealthy are full of violence; your inhabitants speak lies, with tongues of deceit in their mouths.'[3] This, says the prophet Micah, is in stark contrast to God's hope for the people: 'What does the Lord require of you but to do justice, and to love kindness, and to walk humbly with your God?'[4] The desire for justice needs to be embodied in us. So this is where our search for justice needs to be grounded and practised: in our unspectacular daily relationships with friends, neighbours, colleagues and strangers. Walk humbly here with God, practise justice and kindness with your neighbour, and justice will continue to take shape in the wider world, however intimidating the opposition.

Our capacity as human beings for creating injustice seems to be unlimited. The boulder field of injustice stretches beyond our sight. On the other hand our capacity to *Speak Up! Speak Out!* feels limited. Because of this dilemma this practice needs to be lived alongside other practices like *Find Your Stillpoint*[5] and *Live from Your Joy*.[6] The fight against injustice is all the more effective whenever it takes shape within people who have come to recognize their own imbalances, who carry a strong personal sense of peace, and who are already living a life of justice. In this context the struggle against injustice becomes a natural part of who we are. The successes in the fight don't define us, the losses don't deter us. This gives us space to breathe. We can't sign up for every struggle. But we can *Speak Up! Speak Out!* for the struggles into which we are called.

---

3 Micah 6.12.

4 Micah 6.8.

5 Practice 9, 'Find Your Stillpoint'.

6 Practice 28, 'Live from Your Joy'.

Speak Up! Speak Out! A Practice

 An important place to begin *Speak Up! Speak Out!* is to identify the particular struggle(s) for justice that you sense you must be involved in. There may (but not necessarily) be some link to an aspect of your own story. There's something important about ongoing commitment to a particular cause. Work out what your involvement might be. Make a commitment to keep this up for a fixed period of time.

Ai Weiwei says, 'If we don't push, there's nothing happening.' A more just world won't simply happen. It has to begin within us, it has to be pushed for; it has, in the words of Jesus, to hungered and thirsted for. When we do this we may discover that we are not alone, that our own actions are part of a wider movement towards justice, an unstoppable river that will one day see the healing of the nations and the healing of all our injustices.[7] Time to *Speak Up! Speak Out!*

---

7 Revelation 22.1–2.

39

Be with the Forgotten

WE TALK LOSSES

Can I walk with you? and
What are you discussing as you walk along?
We talk losses.
He makes to carry on.
Stay with us . . .

*I was hungry and you gave me food, I was thirsty and you gave me
something to drink, I was a stranger and you welcomed me, I was
naked and you gave me clothing, I was sick and you took care of
me, I was in prison and you visited me.*

A teaching of Jesus: Matthew 25.35–36

Talking Weather, Talking Football

Heh up. How's things? One of the many great things about living
in South Yorkshire as I did for six years was discovering that you
can talk to someone in the queue for your lunchtime breadcake[1]
and not be considered eccentric, weird or dangerous. There's
something vital for the well-being of humanity in the simple act
of looking someone in the face and engaging in conversation. This
simple step into our shared experience (even if we're only talking
about the weather or the football – favourite topics in this part of

---

1 A lovely local word for a bread roll or bap.

the world) reveals something of our deeper connection to each other. We both matter, and this kind of simple interaction between us is both natural and important, a daily remembering of the value and dignity of the human person.

By definition the forgotten people – forgotten around the world and forgotten in your street – are not remembered. As they grow, human societies have always run the risk of remembering only the remembered and forgetting the forgotten. This is nothing new. Currently the initially enticing but ultimately destructive cultures of fame and celebrity are reflecting and fuelling this process. It's so easy to be drawn into a skewed view of the world where being remembered comes from being successful, or where the number of votes, likes or follows we can attract are seen as a sign of pride. But what about those who are not deemed successful, or those whom few vote for, few like or few follow? How can they be brought back into memory – and the world reshaped for good?

Back into the Path of Remembering

The practice of *Be with the Forgotten* is a re-orientation not just of our thoughts, ideas and priorities (although it includes all of those) but of our presence. It's not just a call to *remember* the forgotten but to *be with* the forgotten. Remembering needs to be touched, it needs to be tasted, it needs to be felt. This is a practice that looks to bring peace to the world by uniting the forgotten with the re-membered so that increasingly *all* are remembered. There's a global aspect to this practice, of course. Around the world right now there are countless situations in which people are forgotten. We need to resist the inertia of 'compassion fatigue' and become involved in their remembering. But like all of the practices in *Running Over Rocks*, remembering begins close to home, wherever we are.

A vital contribution of religious communities has been their consistent commitment to remembering the forgotten. Through their own lived-out memory of the remembering Jesus, the hungry have been fed, the thirsty have been given drink, the strangers have been welcomed, the naked have been clothed, the sick have been cared for and the prisoners have been visited.[2] In this emphasis on remembering the forgotten the monastic orders are doing what they have almost always done, calling the institutions who claim to follow Jesus back to the gritty reality of his path. While the resources, time and energy of the churches are inevitably pre-occupied with the issues of the moment, the monastics always urge us back into the heart of the tradition. Towards love of God and love of neighbour. Into prayer and action. Into orientation of ourselves towards the source of being. And into discovery of that divine presence within the discarded and forgotten people around us. This, they show, is what the Jesus path looks like on the ground.

The Remembering Jesus

One way to view the entire wisdom and practice of Jesus is to say that it was all aimed at bringing those who were forgotten back into memory, and thus back into community. So his healing of those suffering from leprosy may be as much about restoring these outcasts to society as it is about relief from a distressing and dangerous disease. In this way Jesus breaks open another society that all too easily remembers the remembered and forgets the for-gotten. He sees and teaches our connectedness. In his teaching, to give food to the forgotten hungry is to feed the Christ, the symbol and means of our connectedness. And it is to be confronted with the uncomfortable reality that *anyone* going hungry can only hap-pen through some act of forgetfulness by wider society – by us, by you and by me. Our forgetting has a real and harmful impact on the people we forget.

Evidence from Jesus' social circle suggests that he confounded any and every attempt to enlist him into one group at the expense of others. His relationships cross all of memory's boundaries. He

---

2 Matthew 25.35–36.

eats with rich officials but allows a despised woman to bathe his feet. He gathers a reputation for hanging around with despised people (despised for a whole variety of deemed offences), but he also befriends the genuinely pious and religious. His disciple group includes an empire-collaborating tax gatherer and a zealot who is conspiring for rebellion. His followers are almost all practising Jews but he asks a despised Samaritan woman for water and muses on the meaning of life with – and learns from – a Syro-Phoenician woman, another people considered to be beyond the pale.

Be with the Forgotten: A Practice

 So how can we begin to *Be with the Forgotten*? In almost every area of your life there will be people who have found themselves consigned to (or who have taken themselves to) the edge of memory or beyond it. Every day we have a choice to be part of their forgetting or part of their remembering. Which path might we choose today?

Make it your practice to regularly sit (or stand or walk or run or eat or drink) with the people in your context whom everyone else ignores – as well as doing the same with the remembered. Perhaps an indication of how we are doing in this earthy practice is to reflect on how often we find ourselves introducing people to each other who would not usually greet each other, never mind engage in conversation or share a breakfast.

Being with the forgotten can take on a particularly effective shape when it is done as a sharing of resources. The Sharing Life Trust based in Oxfordshire is just one fine example of this kind of communal action, a project set up by a group 'who have a passion for community where those who have and can will share their time, energy skills and resources with those who have little and could use some help'.[3] Whenever and wherever the forgotten are remembered the world begins to change for good.

---

3 www.sharinglifetrust.org.

40

Carry Peace with You

REACH OUT YOU CRAZY PEACEMAKER

Reach out beyond what you know
breathe deep into your night fears
and test your ancient-people memories.
Traverse the borders of your tribe
scale the cold face of your doubts
refuse to be walled-in by the hate stories
and shake off the assumptions you have made.
Reach out you crazy peacemaker
and shine.

Blessed are the peacemakers, for they will be called children of God.

A teaching of Jesus: Matthew 5.9

Crazy Peacemakers: The Prisoner and the President

Pace e Bene! I love this Franciscan greeting which means something like 'all peace and good'. It conveys what I hope to offer to those around me and how I aspire to live as a human being in the world. Needless to say, I don't always live out my aspirations. It can come as a shock to discover that *we* may not be quite the peace-filled people that we imagine we are. Tolkien's hobbits may prefer a peaceful life but the history of human beings indicates that we have often chosen a different path. Our capacity for mistrust, fear, anger and occasionally even hate can be extraordinary. But we also have a natural capacity, even I would argue a divine instinct, towards peace-making.

Carry Peace with You is the practice of bringing peace wherever we go. To do this it's vital that we ourselves are people of peace! Words of peace matter but they are only made real through the peaceful, peaceable and peace-making behaviour of which they speak. So peace needs to be nurtured within us. Our peace-intention needs to become peace-making. Like so many practices for a better world in *Running Over Rocks*, this can be costly. Sometimes the story of mistrust between two people, two groups, two teams or two religions can run so deep that peace seems impossible. This kind of scenario almost always requires someone to break ranks, to stretch out the hand of peace (even when they are not the instigators of the breakdown). To become the crazy peacemaker in the manner of the prisoner Nelson Mandela and the president F. W. de Klerk, who risked almost everything as they reached out towards each other with the hope of creating a new and peaceful South Africa. So how can we learn to carry peace within us, and even, should the necessary moment come to us, become the crazy peacemakers who break open years of hostility, fear and mistrust?

Peace to this House

Peace-making is at the heart of the teaching and practice of Jesus. His instructions for his first followers as they prepare to take the great story of divine love further out into the world give a central role to a peace-greeting to be given to every home they may visit: 'Peace to this house.'[1] One of his core sayings, the Beatitudes, places

---

1 Luke 10.5.

peace-making at the heart of his teaching: 'Blessed are the peace-makers, for they will be called children of God.' Whenever you make peace, he seems to be saying, you are fulfilling your role and calling to become what you are meant to be from the beginning of time, to become truly human, to become like children carrying the DNA of your sacred parentage, the ground of your being.

Jesus' first and much-repeated greeting to the Disciples after the crucifixion and resurrection are, according to John, words of peace: 'Peace be with you.'[2] To emphasize the importance of this greeting John records it as being made three times by Jesus. And at this point we may remember that this is the Jesus who forgave his own executioners, and asked us even to love our enemies: 'But I say to you, Love your enemies and pray for those who persecute you.'[3] For Jesus the path to enlightened living – and to a better world – can only be paved with our peaceful actions and our discarded defences.

Abandoning Our Defences

Peace-making requires us to be vulnerable, and sometimes this needs us to stop defending our views, our actions, our possessions, our status, and even – perhaps hardest of all – our reputations. This is of course profoundly counter-intuitive. Look out for the next time you are defending some position or action of yours. The desire to defend rises in us so quickly and so naturally. This may not be wrong in itself. Sometimes if wrong-doing is to be resisted a defensive stance may be needed. Or it may even be helpful if the dialogue helps us to examine what is truly good and right in any situation. But often the taking of defensive positions is far from helpful if we are serious about creating true peace within us and with others. A rapid recourse to defence may actually reveal our immaturity. The mature peacemaker, secure in his or her own

2 John 20.19, 21, 26.
3 Matthew 5.44.

sense of being grounded, has no need to defend a position. In the Jesus tradition this is described as being rooted in Love.[4] When this realization begins to take shape in us, even if in the moment it seems to hurt like hell, in the greater depths of our being we can no longer be hurt.

But the decision to discard our defences is one of the toughest we will ever take. In my experience it's another example of how all of these spiritual practices require continual movement towards what is life-giving. They cannot be achieved, ticked off as done and then forgotten. Every day the call to *Carry Peace with You* requires a new commitment to abandon our defences and take up actions that lead to peace. The very good news is that these practices are not restricted to any (usually false) concept we have of high achievers, the super-spiritual or the exceptionally gifted. The movement towards peaceful actions and abandoned defences is something that we can all make, every day.

Carry Peace with You: A Practice

A good place to begin this practice is to discover some kind of greeting or gesture (or both) that you can embrace that conveys peace (whether that word is used or not). As with any other gesture-practice, such as the one you may use for *Fight Dragons, with Humility*,[5] it's really important for your words and gestures to be true to who you are, and to ring true in your context. First impressions matter. And we are very attuned to the message that people give on first meeting. A host of things are being communicated through our eyes, posture, and attention as well as by our words. The word 'peace' itself carries great potential. See how it sits with you, and how you might use it as or within a greeting. A gesture of open hands conveys a sense of peace (you carry no

---

4 Ephesians 3.18–19.
5 See Practice 34, 'Fight Dragons, with Humility'.

weapon!) and can open up a gesture of peace in the one(s) you are encountering. So an authentic peace-greeting may be a first small step towards a peaceful world. And perhaps the world around us can only become peaceful to the same extent that we are discovering our own sense of peace. This was the teaching of eighteenth-century Russian ascetic St Seraphim of Sarov: 'Acquire inner peace, and thousands around you will find their salvation.' To be shared, peace must be received by us, carried within us, and lived out from us. We need to become the peaceful, peaceable and peace-making people that we long to see around us. A more peaceful world begins with you, and with me, and it begins now!

41

Choose Courageous

LENT (SCRATCHING THE SURFACE)

This season
drives me hard
into my disturbing desert
and keeps me here
confronting stones
scaling pinnacles
exhausting possibilities
in doubts, dreams and hallucinations;
face in the dust
with only the hope of
a third day.

Blessed are those who are persecuted for righteousness' sake, for theirs is the kingdom of heaven.

A teaching of Jesus: Matthew 5.10

With the Peregrine Falcon

I'd love to fly like a bird, but I'm wary of heights. So I'm open-mouthed watching the amazing footage on YouTube of wingsuit flyers jumping off mountains, following but avoiding (they and we hope) the contours of the cliffs. My enjoyment of this is of course strictly vicarious! It's enough for me to stand on a cliff-top above the River Avon by the Clifton Suspension Bridge in Bristol. To be just a waist-high metal fence away from a drop of a few hundred feet down to the gorge below, and to imagine that my view is being shared with the elusive peregrine falcon, is an exhilarating experience. Whenever I stand there my love of the sensation is helping me to overcome my fear of the height. In some very small way I suppose I'm choosing to be courageous.

Sooner or later in every human life there comes a moment, a day or a season when it's clear that on a much bigger scale, only courage will see us through. This is part of the earthy reality of what it means to be human. And deciding to *Choose Courageous* in the face of immense difficulty is part of the key to discovering peace for ourselves, and thus key to the bringing of peace to the world around us. The ability to make this choice is deep within all of us. It's not about having no fear. That would be unreal and foolish. Our sense of fear is there to protect us, and in some situations flight from fear is absolutely the right thing to do. The problem is that fear can begin to characterize how we view the world, everything we do, and even what we become. The practice of *Choose Courageous* is about learning to accept our fear and finding what we need to continue along the good path that offers itself to us.

Doing the Right Thing

One core element in the discovery of courage is making the decision to do the right thing, whatever the cost. There's something very freeing and beautiful about making a decision to do this. To reject anything that could compromise our commitment to the spirit in which we ground ourselves[1] is one of the most important steps towards maturity that we will ever take. In his teaching Jesus keeps returning to a word which we translate as 'Blessed'[2] and

---

1 See Practice 30, 'Stay in Your Spirit'.
2 The Beatitudes in Matthew 5.1–12 and Luke 6.20–23.

usually pronounce as 'bless-ed' – conveying in the sound a sense of movement. In the wisdom of Jesus, being bless-ed comes from doing the right thing, whatever the personal cost, even if it leads to our 'persecution'. And to do this *will* almost inevitably be a costly experience that will in some way affect our status, our pocket, or our popularity. But it will also bring its own deep enlightenment.

In committing ourselves to doing the right thing whatever the cost, we will begin to experience the bliss of what Jesus calls the 'kingdom of heaven' – that state of everything good flourishing here and now. In the south-west peninsula of England there are occasional days far into autumn when the sun will take you by surprise in its warmth and depth of light. After days of cloud and rain, we'll take the light here whenever it comes, and just to stand for a few moments, eyes closed, face lifted towards the sun is a wonderful experience. This is what doing the right thing feels like. The winter will still need to be negotiated. That hasn't changed. But the last flicker of summer-warmth in autumn is a reminder that the sun is still around, and will continue to be around, and that, one day, spring will return.

The Climbing Frame and the Courageous Cosmos

My fear of heights has rebounded on others. I've been trying to remember if I encouraged our children when they were small to climb to the very top of the climbing frame in the local park. Was I saying 'Go for it!' or was my message 'Be careful!'? Their consensus now is that it was probably a mix of both. I have a feeling that I may have erred too much on the side of 'be careful'. Our fear that someone we love might become hurt is understandable. But I wonder if that fear can mean that we hold them back from becoming the truly courageously human people they want and need to become. Perhaps we and they will only learn about falling, and about our capacity to recover from the fall, by falling? This requires another kind of courage, not so much for ourselves but for others: the courage to let them discover life for themselves – in all its complexity, mess and wonder.

Whatever the context of our seeking to *Choose Courageous*, there's another vital gift of the Jesus tradition in its understanding that every small act of courage is both an affirmation of the ultimate goodness of existence, and a personal experience of that goodness. In one of the most famous stories Jesus tells – the story of the brother who squanders his inheritance[3] (a story full of fear and courage, both at times misplaced) – all the decisions made, however poor, fade into insignificance when we encounter the boy's father running towards the son who was lost, arms outstretched in welcome. The boy's courage and fear are both gathered up in a loving embrace. The destiny of everything, despite appearances, is good, and whenever we *Choose Courageous* we are stepping into that great stream of goodness. This is what parents are doing every time they consciously bring a child into a tough world in tough times. Theirs is an act of courageous participation in a courageous cosmos – and a statement of desire, hope and belief that somehow everything *will* be well.

Choose Courageous: A Practice

 Like most of the practices in *Running Over Rocks*, the practice of *Choose Courageous* is grounded in self-awareness. Try to notice the next situation, choice or dilemma in which a courageous response might be an option for you. Catch yourself beginning to make a decision. Ask yourself: What might be the truly courageous option here? What might doing the right thing look like? And so may you *Choose Courageous* and may the world be changed.

---

3 Luke 15.11–32.

42

Become the Deep Change

LIGHT A CANDLE (TO START A FIRE)

You could take a sledge-hammer to this place.
You could begin to knock it down.
And drag the furniture into the street.
Build a pyre. Pour on petrol.
Then light a great fire.
Stand well back.
And see it burn.

Or you could light a candle.
You could put it in a jar.
And carry it with you to your neighbour.
Ask your neighbour to do the same.
Then move in close.
And find yourself
all flame.

*The kingdom of heaven is like yeast that a woman took and mixed
in with three measures of flour until all of it was leavened.*

A parable of Jesus: Matthew 13.33

Bonfire of the Successes

Imagine that all the best work you have ever done, and all the best work you ever will do, is somehow collected in one place. The work includes all your best efforts, all your most insightful ideas and all your finest actions. Nothing good is missed. Everything is here in this one place. And today all the people you love and respect are beginning to gather from all over to experience and celebrate this great collection with you tomorrow. But in a tragic incident overnight the building where the work has been brought together is engulfed in a massive fire. No-one is hurt but all your work and all record of it is destroyed, and only a few barely recognizable fragments remain. Shocked at the news of what has happened, the people begin to turn up in the morning, and in time everyone who was invited is there. All you have is your family, your friends, these people whom you have worked with and for, and the clothes you stand up in. Tearfully you thank people for coming. One by one, as the last wisps of smoke rise from this bonfire of your successes, they begin to speak.

I wonder if the *kind of people we are* in life is at least as important as *any legacy of work* we leave to the world? *Both* matter. I can think of a number of artists from different eras and in different fields, all producing greatly respected and much-loved work, but who apparently were or are not so great to be around. I would be so disappointed to be without access to their body of work. Would their work lack the edge it actually has if they were more joyful to be around? Possibly, we might imagine, but not necessarily. So perhaps a different, and genuine, question needs to be asked. How can the artist live up to the greatest aspirations of his or her art, and to the greater truth that the art is revealing? And how might any of us live up to the aspirations of our art, of our work, of our calling? In some senses the creating of the art, the making of the work is the easy bit. The real challenge is living it in the context of the ordinary but extraordinary fellow human beings all around us. We must embody our work in ourselves. In Mahatma Gandhi's famous phrase, we must become the change we want to see in the world.

Small Steps, Unseen Experiments

How does the world get changed for the better? Most big changes come in small steps, through unseen experiments, and from intuitive innovations. Few of us may be in a position to be at the centre of the huge landmark changes that shift society – so it's vital that we are open to working in ways that are small, local, hidden, unnoticed and deep. If bigness comes our way, if a wider reputation emerges, if 'success' happens in our change-making, let it come by all means. But it seems to me that there is great wisdom in not seeking bigness, in treating reputation with great caution, and being wary of the allure of success.

The practice of *Become the Deep Change* is about embracing a life of depth – being willing to be low-profile, even at times hidden from sight, unconcerned for any fluctuations in standing, popularity or honour. It's also about seeking depth in the sense of weight, character and long-term commitment – the opposite of being shallow, bland, manipulative or fickle. But perhaps most importantly it's about embodying the change we seek. Our work and our character need to accompany each other, and there's a problem when either gets left behind. One way we'll be ignoring our creativity, the other we'll be confining our vision to our work and forgetting that the way we live speaks as loudly as any of it.

The Lesson of Yeast

What might happen if we commit to nurturing low-profile ways of life in which bringing goodness is the main priority, regardless of reputation, status or success? I'm aware of an irony present in musing on this possibility while hoping that this book and my other work continue to reach out to wider audiences (and them to me). But whatever the outcome of this work, there is great freedom in sensing that I'm creating what I think I am called to create, and doing what I'm meant to do, and that the work's impact is not for me to speculate on, worry about, or even be proud of.

Jesus teaches about bread-making.[1] Actually, he's not teaching bread-making but teaching *from* bread-making. He focuses on yeast, the key ingredient, small, unpromising, and hidden deep in the process. The gift(s) you have – and you have gifts – are a kind of yeast for the world. Yeast needs hiddenness to do its yeasty thing. There may be more high-profile ingredients in bread. But yeast is vital. So may we value the small, the unpromising, the hidden.

Become the Deep Change: A Practice

 This practice will involve you in resistance and imagination. In the United Kingdom at this time I sense that there's something destructive going on in the privatization of public services. A campaign is under way, orchestrated or otherwise – you decide which – to encourage us to get to a point where we find ourselves accepting that privatization is the only option, and indeed the 'normal' state of things. It is of course neither.

Resistance to this kind of change will require a lot of us. The arguments will need to be made – our work, if you like. But just as important will be the way that we imagine and then embody alternative possibilities, laughing as we refuse to accept the unacceptable, joyfully offering other possibilities. A way into this practice: decide to do something good every day this week, whether or not anyone will see it being done. *Become the Deep Change!*

---

1 Matthew 13.33.

PRACTICES OF THE BELOVED LIFE

From absence towards presence: the Jesus path

A much-loved cross from Ethiopia, a gift from a friend but lost one day when the cord came loose. May it always be a gift to the finder.

The next series of practices is at the heart of the ancient and unfolding Jesus tradition. They are long tried and much tested. Together they form a pattern of movement from absence to presence. At their heart lies the possibility that, amazingly, the Christ is not just an idea but a personal and universal presence. The shape and look of these practices will vary from place to place, and from time to time, but their essence remains the same.

Whatever your own human journey, I hope that in encountering them – even for the first time – they may feel like gifts. If you place yourself *within* the Jesus tradition I hope that they might inspire you to continue on that path. I also hope that in some small way they might provoke a wider interest in spiritual (and therefore human) formation in the way of the teacher Jesus.

The practices here are called Beloved Life for a number of reasons closely connected to the Jesus tradition. The relationship between Lover and Beloved is at the heart of the Song of Songs, one of the great texts of the Jewish faith that formed Jesus, inspired the Gospel writers and fired the imagination of mystics such as St John of the Cross. At the beginning of Jesus' public life, in his baptism in the wilderness by John the Baptizer, a voice is heard from heaven calling Jesus the Beloved. This happens again on the mountain at the Transfiguration. Jesus himself uses the phrase in one of his parables. And in the early Church the term Beloved began to be used to describe the followers of Jesus. In the light of these connections and their implications, I suggest that our sense of being beloved may be essential if we are to bring love – and goodness in all its forms – to the world.

Each of the practices in this series is offered in two stages. The first draws on the principle of the practice, to offer a way to live in its spirit where you are. The second offers a way into the traditional practice itself. These practices are all being explored in Beloved Life – a project of spiritual practice based in the south-west of England.[1]

The season connected with these Practices of the Beloved Life is All Saints and the period before Advent known as Kingdom. At All Saints the tradition celebrates our place in the long story of those who have tried to follow the path of Jesus over the centuries. In the Kingdom season the tradition reminds us that the saints are never focused in on themselves, but always looking for the good reshaping of the world in the way of the Christ.

---

1 See www.belovedlife.org for more on Beloved Life and for resources connected to these practices.

43

Eucharist (Taste Paradise)

EATING FLOWERS

Yesterday I was eating flowers
(don't try this at home)
a strange and subtle feast
of orange blue sea-green
a machair meadow with scallops, mussels and clams –
a counter-intuitive return to Eden.
Yesterday I was eating flowers.

(*Machair* is a Gaelic word describing the fields of shell-sand at the Atlantic coastal edges of the Scottish mainland and the Western Isles.)

When the hour came, (Jesus) took his place at the table, and the apostles with him. He said to them, 'I have eagerly desired to eat this Passover with you before I suffer.'

From the life of Jesus: Luke 22.14–15

Taste of Paradise

'Welcome to paradise!' This is not the usual greeting at the beginning of any Eucharist. But I believe that it (or something like it) could have been the greeting at any time in the first thousand years of the life of the Church, and could be so again. The Eucharist – the Mass, the Holy Communion, the Lord's Supper, the Breaking of Bread – is perhaps the central and defining act of communal Christian worship and spirituality across the main traditions and denominations. So it matters, deeply. In their brilliant and detailed book[1] exploring the early history of the Christian faith, Rita Nakashima Brock and Rebecca Ann Parker suggest that we have forgotten the central meaning of the Eucharist. Its *primary* meaning is not as a solemn memorial of the redemptive death of Jesus but as a revelation of the paradise that Jesus worked for, taught about (describing it as the kingdom of heaven), embodied in himself, and pointed out as being already both within us and all around us. However tough life gets – for us, our neighbour and the planet – the possibility of paradise, declares the practice of Eucharist, is already here, breaking in and breaking out all around us!

So to share in the Eucharist (which means 'Thanksgiving') is to enter a joyful feast that reveals the connection and goodness of humanity, earth and God. In the parish church where I was curate one of the most important things we did was to go through the process of enabling children to receive the Eucharist before confirmation (the usual Anglican process is to make children wait until after confirmation). In one of the public meetings needed to make sure that all views were being heard one parishioner asked what we would do if a child, not understanding the solemnity of the service, might run up the aisle to receive the communion. In that moment it was as if we could hear the sounds of pennies dropping and people thinking – shouldn't we *all* be running up every week to receive the bread of life and the wine of salvation – a taste of paradise!

Hospitality and Home-coming

One of the happy discoveries that we make about Jesus in the Gospels is his fondness for eating and drinking with people. Particularly with the 'wrong' people – cheating bosses, shamed

1 Rita Nakashima Brock and Rebecca Ann Parker, *Saving Paradise: How Christianity Traded Love of This World for Crucifixion and Empire*, London: Canterbury Press, 2012.

prostitutes, despised foreigners and supposed sinners of all kinds. His first miracle, the Gospel writer John tells us, is his contribution to the marriage feast at Cana of Galilee. Here he changes water into wine (apparently in huge quantities). The offering of hospitality has continued to be one of the finest marks of the community of spiritual practice that evolved in the way and name of Jesus.

The Gospel writers confirm that the early Church – those first groups of followers of the Jesus path who gathered after his death, resurrection and ascension – were particularly interested in offering hospitality. Their practice, and the Eucharist that has emerged from their early experience, reveal a hospitality that is given without any sense of obligation. The only thing that the Eucharist demands of us is authenticity in our desire to be involved in reshaping ourselves and the world for good. In the same way I think that there's a case for saying to our house guests 'bring nothing' rather than 'bring a bottle'. The Eucharist is a joyful home-coming!

Presence and the Kiss

The Eucharist is also about presence. There's long been controversy within the broader Christian tradition around what actually happens to the bread and wine during the Eucharist. Perhaps the most important thing is that somehow, mysteriously, however it happens, in the act of sharing in the Eucharist, the divine community is experienced as being present to us. And we in turn are moved to become present to the God who in Jesus the Christ comes to us.

The Eucharist both symbolizes and mediates (discloses, makes real, enables) in a particular space and in a particular moment what is going on everywhere all the time – our deep at-oneness with God. The Eucharist, we might say, is like the lovers' kiss or love-making. In any love relationship these moments, at their best, are intimate signs in particular moments of an all-the-time love.

These acts also mediate the love to which they point, enabling that love to flourish and deepen.

So in the paradise of the eucharistic kiss the depth of divine love for us is revealed, and our own instinctive (but sometimes forgotten) all-the-time love for God and for the cosmos is given shape and new life. Furthermore, the experience of the tradition in the Eucharist is that it reveals to us the presence of God in the world around us. As we experience the divine presence in the sharing of the bread and wine of the Eucharist, we may begin to recognize the aroma and taste of divine presence all around us.

Eucharist (Taste Paradise): A Practice

A way into a practice of *Eucharist (Taste Paradise)* that draws on the spirit of the tradition is to open up your table. Invite some friends and their friends to a meal. Be ready to include someone you don't know well. Breakfast can be a great meal to do this – there's much less pressure to produce something astonishing, and there's great precedent in the tradition[2] for this. This meal, you may discover, can be full of the eucharistic spirit – a place of thanksgiving, a taste of paradise, a hospitable home-coming, an experience of presence.

The practice of the Eucharist itself may be more complicated. Not every church allows everyone to receive the bread and wine. And perhaps not every Eucharist feels like a taste of paradise. If that's your experience I apologize. But I encourage you to find a way to enter into this practice. Seek out someone you know who is trying to live in the Jesus tradition, and find out whether their practice of Eucharist might be calling you. Persist in your quest to respond to Jesus' own invitation. Welcome to paradise!

---

2 The risen Jesus invites the Disciples for an early morning breakfast on the beach: John 21.12.

44

Pilgrimage (On the Road)

EVEN THE COLD RAIN

Why am I doing this?
To test myself, an idea, a theory
to remember a dream, a memory, a story
to forget a lie, a loss, a humiliation
to confess a betrayal, a wrong, a compulsion
to discover a path, a possibility, a truth
to uncover a lover, a friend, a life?

No matter. Everything finds its place.
There are no wrong motives for walking
three hundred miles or thirty or even three.
I begin to sink and sync into the landscape
and let the questions fall away.
It may be all gift. Even the cold rain.

*Take no gold, or silver, or copper in your belts, no bag for your
journey, or two tunics, or sandals, or a staff; for labourers deserve
their food.*

Instructions of Jesus to the twelve apostles: Matthew 10.9–10

Walking with Our Fears

Hallelujah Saint Birinus!
Hallelujah Saint Birinus!

One of the highlights of the ecumenical Church year, celebrated by all the churches in Oxfordshire, is the St Birinus pilgrimage from Churn Knob near Blewberry to the abbey at Dorchester-on-Thames. This annual pilgrimage on a Sunday in early July remembers a local hero, St Birinus, who in the seventh century preached to the West Saxons and baptized their king Cynegils. To walk with a few hundred others, young and old, booted walkers and unprepared first-timers, all sharing a common desire to follow the Christ in the footsteps of this long-remembered local saint, is an amazing experience. The repeated shout, 'Hallelujah St Birinus!' marks the noisy highpoint of the service in the abbey at the end of the pilgrimage walk. As we gather around the shrine there's a palpable sense that the saint and all the company of heaven are with us now. However bad things have been in the previous months, whatever our fears for the future, we were not, and never will be, alone!

Pilgrimage is a physical journey made with spiritual intention. And it's this mix of physicality and spirituality that makes the practice of pilgrimage such a vital one in the tradition. Physical capability is not enough on pilgrimage. Belief alone is not enough. Experience on its own won't carry us through. Even desire is not enough. Rather, it's the coming together of all these characteristics of what it means to be human in the world that makes a pilgrimage experience and enables it to shape us for good.

Walking with Our Questions

The physical journey begins to reveal something of our greater journeys though life. And the questions raised by the physical journey begin to work on us – the sort of questions that produced the poem 'Even the cold rain', and questions like: Can I do this? Why am I doing this? and, of course, How can I walk with these crazy people? (My answer: only because I too am crazy.) Every aspect of the experience contributes to the shaping nature of pilgrimage. The people we meet and the privations we share. The stuff we leave behind and the baggage we take. The difficult encounters and the joyful surprises along the way.

The 2011 film *The Way*, written and directed by Emilio Estevez and featuring his father Martin Sheen in the lead role, is a wonderful exploration of the possibility of pilgrimage. The story unfolds around the Camino de Santiago de Compostela, the network of famous pilgrimage routes that begin in the French Pyrenees, wind through the Basque area of northern Spain and conclude at the tomb of Jesus' disciple St James in Santiago. Never sentimental, always honest and inspiring, the film opens up the demands of making a pilgrimage, but reveals the gritty wonder of what such an endeavour might reveal and do to us.

Pilgrimage has roots both in the practice of the Jewish faith and in the practice of Jesus himself, who famously went missing on the way home to Galilee from his community's annual pilgrimage to the Temple in Jerusalem to make sacrifices.[1] As an adult, Jesus seems to have walked to Jerusalem more than once. And this teacher-pilgrim seems to have understood that pilgrimage is best done by travelling light. There's only so much food, water and shelter the pilgrim can carry with him or her, and so the pilgrim needs to learn to be reliant on others for some of the basic necessities for the journey. Jesus' instructions to his own Disciples as they are about to set out on a walking pilgrimage to share the good news of his message are clear: 'Take no gold, or silver, or copper in your belts, no bag for your journey, or two tunics, or sandals, or a staff'.[2] We need to be able to trust the journey, trust those we meet, and trust the God on whose good earth we walk.

---

1 Luke 2.41–52.
2 Matthew 10.9–10.

Walking with Our Desires

We make pilgrimage for all kinds of reasons. Almost none of them are wrong. What matters is our willingness to look those reasons in the eye. There will, after all, be plenty of time to face them as we walk. One of the most common changes that seems to happen to us on pilgrimage is a kind of sifting for what truly matters. This can be painful (initially – and often), humiliating (as we pay attention to our thought patterns), and eventually even welcome (if we persist in our desire to learn and be changed).

Our desires begin to loom large. Boot on road, sun on skin, pack on back and water on tongue become our physical priorities, and some of the many other concerns to which we are normally drawn begin to fade away, swallowed by the landscape. Our relationships with fellow pilgrims begin to reveal what we really think (for better and for worse) of other people. Our desire for God, our desire for another, our desire for life itself, begin to emerge from the chaos of conflicting desires that have been battling it out within us. We may even hear again a question that Jesus asked of someone else on the road: 'What do you want me to do for you?'[3]

Pilgrimage (On the Road): A Practice

The first stage of the practice *Pilgrimage (On the Road)* is a commitment to live with the spirit of pilgrimage. To become willing to see your life right now as a journey, to travel light, to commit to learning from whatever happens on the way, to keep going. And to be changed.

The second stage involves making a pilgrimage in the ancient Jesus tradition. There are lots of resources and ways into this. Do some research – what might be the local pilgrim routes where you are? If there appear to be none, might it be that you are called to

3 Luke 18.41.

begin one, perhaps to celebrate a local saint, or a local incident of God's blessing? The Diocese of Oxford publishes a pilgrimage map showing pilgrim trails across the diocese, including the route of the St Birinus pilgrimage.[4] And the Bishop of Oxford has written a pocket book of prayers for pilgrims.[5] A note of caution: if you are not used to walking longer distances, make sure you find something that you sense will be manageable for you. And a note of adventure: Get out *On the Road*! Become a pilgrim! You will be changed for good, and as you walk through and into that change, so will the world around you.

---

4 www.oxford.anglican.org.

5 John Pritchard, *Pocket Prayers for Pilgrims*, London: Canterbury Press, 2011.

45

Lectio Divina (Free the Words)

A WILD SWIM WITH MAYFLIES

Sliding into the cold stream
over booming boulder stones,
slipping their uncertain foothold
the current carries me further
into the river's flow
out into sunlight
shimmering on the rippled surface
amongst mayflies in their short abundant dance
their Mary's wild and precious life
their delirious path of love.

Gratefully I am carried
into the stillness of a clear deep pool.
Floating and held. Gazing and being gazed upon.
I laugh. I had tried to read the river.
But the river read me, asking
how will you live your
mayfly life?

(The phrase 'wild and precious life' is from the poetry of Mary Oliver.)

They said to each other, 'Were not our hearts burning within us while he was talking to us on the road, while he was opening the scriptures to us?'

From the life of Jesus: Luke 24.32

World-changing Words

Words can change worlds. In just a few printed shapes, in a few uttered sounds, and in the pregnant spaces between them, new possibilities emerge. The scripture-words of the Jesus tradition have done their fair share of changing worlds, often (but not always) for good. The Jewish and Christian approach to Scripture is similar (and of course they share many texts – the Christian Old Testament borrows most of the Jewish scriptures). They both have a sense that the Scriptures are not just words, or even ideas, but that somehow they continue to offer new truth and insight. An early follower of Jesus (and Jewish-faith scholar) described them as 'God-breathed'.[1] And for the attentive reader, for the listener with an open heart, the divine breath can still be sensed now. Perhaps once again we need to *Free the Words* to let them do their thing in us.

Earlier in the book I introduced the practice of *Close-up (Terra Divina)*.[2] Here I want to go back to the roots of that practice, to Lectio Divina, the monastic practice of 'sacred reading' of the great texts of the Judaeo-Christian faith. I've been experimenting with this for around ten years and I continue to be excited about its potential for putting the great texts of faith back in the hands and hearts of the people. Lectio Divina is a way of receiving the text so that it is not so much about *information* as *formation*. It's not so much about shaping our ideas and our beliefs (as important and helpful as they are) as about shaping our whole being – body, mind and spirit. 'How might this scripture shape me and the way I live today?' is the kind of question that Lectio Divina provokes in us. Or, 'How might the wisdom, insight or toughness of this passage change me today?'

---

1 St Paul in 2 Timothy 3.16.
2 See Practice 3, 'Close-up (Terra Divina)'.

Lectio Divina

This is my own practice of Lectio Divina. This is best done in a set-ting that allows you to focus, as much as possible, on this alone, if only for a few minutes.

Step one is *lectio* – the reading. Here we are trying to sense the gift that the scripture may be offering us. Read the chosen passage two or three times. Receive the text as it comes. Forget what you may think you know about it. Let a word, phrase or idea catch your attention. Then take your time with it. Let it sit with you, and you with it.

Step two is *meditatio* – the meditation. Here we are engaging with the text in thinking mode. Begin to wonder why whatever has caught your attention might have done so, and wonder why it might be a gift to you. What might be the truth or wisdom that the scripture wants to share with you? The gift may be a challenging one, but we can trust that there is some giftedness within it.

Step three is *oratio* – the prayer or the yearning. This is where we let the text do its work on us and through us. If you pray, let whatever has caught your attention carry your prayers at this time. If you see yourself as someone who hopes or yearns rather than prays, let your hopes and yearnings be carried by it. As things come to mind that are concerning you let them be carried by the idea, phrase or word. Try simply repeating the phrase silently, letting it do the work of concern or hope.

Step four is *contemplatio* – contemplation or presence.[3] This may feel like sweet liberation. It can also feel as if nothing has changed. Either way, go with it. Let go of whatever has caught your atten-tion. Enjoy the sense of being alive, of being held, of being at one

3 See Practice 46, 'Cave of the Heart (Nurture your Contemplative)'.

with everything. Some experience this as being held in a benevolent universe. In the Jesus tradition this is experienced as somehow being in the presence of the community of God, the Holy Trinity.

The Girl on the Bus

We carry words with us. Words we've heard, words we've read, or words we've said ourselves all accompany us. Some of them will of course be hurtful and difficult. I wish I could forget what the girl on the bus said to me on the way home from school one day! But decades later it's still there, somewhere deep in the background, in a box labelled 'fragile'. Ironically, of course, she had probably forgotten what she said within a minute. But our remembered words can also be an amazing source for good within us. So when you practise Lectio Divina, let the gifted words find a place in you, repeat them, memorize them and carry them with you.

A note of caution. Just very occasionally I find that someone will sift and shred the text for what they really want – or really don't want – to hear. They'll ignore the wider sense of the passage, and even remove the words that clarify or shape the context, so that up becomes down, light becomes dark and good becomes one of its many opposites. So whenever I'm doing this in a group context I'll always offer a brief suggestion of the wider context of the passage, and include a reference to how the community of the tradition has broadly understood the direction of the text over the centuries. And I'll remind everyone that we bring ourselves to the text, just as the text comes to us.

Lectio Divina (Free the Words): A Practice

 The first stage of the practice of *Lectio Divina (Free the Words)* in the spirit of Lectio Divina is to develop an awareness of the words and ideas that are shaping you. What words have caught your attention today? What ideas are you excited about at this time?

The second stage is to develop your own practice of Lectio Divina. Follow the guidelines here. You can work your way through a longer passage of Scripture by reading just a few verses each time you do the practice. If anything, read less rather than more. This can, of course, be done in company, and it can be particularly insightful to do this as part of a regular group gathering. The words we read, the phrases we hear and the brief silences between come to us echoing down the centuries, full of God-breathed possibility. *Free the Words!*

46

Cave of the Heart
(Nurture Your Contemplative)

I AM A BREATH

I am a breath, a ripple, a drop of rain.
A flicker, a word, a look, a name.

With its silence and heat
the desert strips away all
your pretence, your defence, your sense
of what is important or true; and leaves
you musing on lizards and beetles,
on rocks and soil, on clouds and sky.

So sit you shuffling buddha stay
in time your stuff may begin to fall away.
Nothing spectacular, perhaps
no peace transcendent,
no garden state of enlightenment
but a shift or drift that is curiously good,
revealing the at-oneness of all that is.

I am a breath, a ripple, a drop of rain.
A flicker, a word, a look, a name.

Remember, I am with you always, to the end of the age.

A teaching of Jesus: Matthew 28.20b

Contemplative Zippo

The opening, the taking, the tapping, the bringing up, the lighting, the drawing in, the breathing out, the watching, and the letting go. There's a contemplative in everyone. And for this young and unknowing contemplative, the reassuring clunk and smell of the Zippo further heightened the experience. I'm not advocating that we should all return to the contemplative ritual of the mid-morning cigarette with our coffee. But I am suggesting that the ability and desire to pause, to become still, and to remain in the place that is beyond what we can see may just be our natural home.

It's disappointing that the followers of Jesus have not always been noted for their contemplative approach to life. We've often been (towards our worst) more concerned about right beliefs and correct behaviours, or (closer to our best) focused on actions to make a better world. But the contemplative strand has always been present at the heart of the Jesus tradition. It is the necessary starting point for any real change for good to take shape in us and then ripple out into the wider world. And it comes to us directly from the life and practice of Jesus himself. The contemplative or mystical path has always been with us – loved, guarded and practised by a few, particularly by the monastics. To many it has remained a hidden secret – but thankfully it is now beginning to re-emerge. This is the vital practice of *Cave of the Heart (Nurture Your Contemplative)*.

Happening to, Being with

So what's happening in contemplation? I've already suggested that it is the act of locating and then living at our stillpoint.[1] It can also be understood and encountered in the final stage in the practice of Sacred Reading, where we let go of the words – both of the text

---

1 See Practice 9, 'Find Your Stillpoint'.

of Scripture in Lectio Divina[2] and of the wisdom of the earth in *Close-up (Terra Divina)*.[3]

Another idea I find helpful is to think of it as the divine, the mystery or God *happening to us*.[4] That rings true in my experience, suggesting the possibility that prayer (and here I'm using the words prayer and contemplation as pointing towards the same experience) may be at God's initiative rather than ours, with therefore an inherent possibility of surprise, a sense that this is just the start of something that may unfold with profound effects, something that may stop us in our tracks: like a burning bush, a wrestling stranger, or the stillness after a storm, an earthquake and a fire.[5]

Developing this possibility further, the tradition also experiences the *happening to us* of contemplation as a simple but profound *being with*. There's a dramatic story told in the Gospels of a boat carrying the Disciples of Jesus across the lake of Galilee.[6] It's night-time and a huge storm suddenly blows up. Jesus is asleep in the stern; the frightened Disciples wake him to save them. His response – 'Why are you afraid? Have you still no faith?' – suggests that his being with them would have been enough. And later, at the very end of Matthew's account of Jesus' life, his final words to the Disciples are recorded as being a promise to be with us always.[7] This, his presence, is all we need.

Re-orienting Ourselves, Redrawing the Circle

Now of course *being with* someone takes time for the *being with* to reveal the true wonder of the connection. *Being with* can actually be very difficult. Imagine yourself in a lift with someone unknown to you. It feels strange and awkward. The floor suddenly becomes

---

2 See Practice 45, 'Free the Words'.
3 See Practice 3, 'Close-up (Terra Divina)'.
4 I'm grateful to Fr David Cherry for this phrase.
5 Biblical images from some of the oldest parts of the Jewish faith.
6 See Mark 4.35–41 and Matthew 8.23–27.
7 Matthew 28.20.

very interesting. But now imagine yourself sitting in a room with someone you love, like your partner or spouse, or a close friend. Here the silence and stillness are fine – a shared experience that somehow connects you. This is how contemplation can be. Words may be said but no words are necessary. There is no anxiety. No fear. Only love and acceptance.

So: contemplation as God *happening to us* and as *being with*. Here's another perspective: contemplation as *re-orienting ourselves*. In *Cave Refectory Road* I suggested a centring practice that I called 'Meister Eckhart's Circle'.[8] I based this on an insight from Meister Eckhart von Hochheim, a medieval Dominican friar and professor of theology. Eckhart suggested that to live well we need to find and keep to a central pivot point, 'like', he said, 'a person drawing a circle'. Now of course most of the time we live where the action is, on the fast-moving edge of the circle. That's how life is and it's OK as far as it goes. But the problem is that we all too easily lose our centre, our stillpoint, our located-ness in our place of belonging in the life of God. We need to redraw that circle. To find the centre, and keep it so. A daily practice of contemplation is a daily drawing of the circle, a daily finding of that still centre.

Cave of the Heart (Nurture Your Contemplative): A Practice

I'll be bold enough to say that some practice of *Cave of the Heart (Nurture Your Contemplative)* is essential for anyone who is serious about becoming truly human. But in my experience there are also some people who have a particular capacity and calling to live deeply in and from the contemplative path. And I want to suggest that every community needs a contemplative (or more than one!). And so does every project, every business, every

8 Ian Adams, *Cave Refectory Road: Monastic Rhythms for Contemporary Living*, London: Canterbury Press, 2010, pp. 40–2.

venture, every organization, and every decision-making body. Our contemplatives provide the necessary counter-balance to all our words and activity. More importantly, if given space, they provide the starting point for almost anything good that can be accomplished by the group. This need not be a fanciful idea. What amazing things might happen if the organizations of which we are part began to make it a priority to nurture the contemplative?

So this is the stance of *Cave of the Heart (Nurture Your Contemplative)*. At the first stage, in the spirit of the tradition's ancient practice of contemplation, this is about developing your own stance of stillness, presence, and openness to all that exists. Drawing on the resources in *Running Over Rocks*, find a way into the practice that works for you.[9]

At the second stage, find a guide in the contemplative path who practises from within the ancient and unfolding Jesus tradition.[10] Let their experience help you to re-orientate yourself. And may the source of their experience, the dynamic community of God whom the tradition encounters as loving Father–Mother, contemplative Christ and joyful Spirit, happen to you, be with you, and become your point of orientation, each day and always.

9 For ideas see Practices 8, 'Slow into Stillness', 9, 'Find Your StillPoint', 3, 'Close-up (Terra Divina)', and 45, 'Free the Words'.

10 See www.belovedlife.org and www.thestillpoint.org.uk for suggestions for possible guides.

47

Reconciliation
(Reconcile, be Reconciled)

MOUTH IN THE DUST

This is the view from the ground
this is my lamentation
this is life.

Mouth in the dust
bleeding lips
bruised forehead
broken ribs
scuffed skin.

Where are you?

Forgive, and you will be forgiven.

A teaching of Jesus: Luke 6.37b

Breaking the Shame and Blame Impulse

There will be no miracles here. I love Nathan Coley's art installation
of this name in the gardens of the Scottish National Gallery of
Modern Art Two in Edinburgh. I spent an hour with this installation towards dusk one November afternoon, as the lights that

form the words on a large structure of scaffolding gradually became more prominent. I like the way the words say one thing
(*There will be no miracles here*) while, for me at least, they also
seem to ask a question (*But could there be miracles here?*). In the
areas of broken human relationships (of all types) and the need for
reconciliation, these two phrases are, it seems to me, vital. On the
one hand, the reality of our fractures must be faced. But we cannot
lose the hope that our breakages might find healing.

A particular concern at the moment is the extent to which we
seem to be in thrall to the destructive twin powers of *shame and
blame*. Whatever the mistake, crisis or disaster, our desire to find
someone to scapegoat seems to be very strong. I sense that this is
often a search for someone onto whom we can transfer some of our
own shame, a search for someone whose wrong-doing (we con-
vince ourselves) is always greater than our own. This destructive
cycle of shame and blame is a problem, and it needs addressing. I
hope that the practice of *Reconciliation (Reconcile, be Reconciled)*
may be one step in this direction.

The Landscape of Reconciliation

The possibility of a deep reconciliation that deals with shame and
blame runs through Jesus' teaching and practice. His focus seems
to be on the restoring of communion with other human beings,
with the earth and with God. If reconciliation is for Jesus always
the bigger picture, the starting point is often around some act of
forgiveness – and in turn forgiveness becomes part of something
much bigger. So the smallest act of forgiveness is a re-imagining
and remaking of the world! And there can be no limits to the scope
of reconciliation. Indeed, nothing that is broken or damaged can
be off limits.

If the potential reach of reconciliation sparked by forgiveness
is always larger than we might imagine, it always needs to begin
in a coming home to ourselves. It really is only possible to truly

forgive others when we forgive ourselves. Once we manage to do this we are on the road to forgiving others. Then we have to *become* and *embody* forgiveness and reconciliation, so that they aren't just things we do but *something we are*! We have to become reconciled people to bring reconciliation. And we can only go on being reconciled if we are reconciling with others. This is the virtuous circle of reconciliation in the way of Jesus. This is the way that forgiveness works, passed on from one to another. This is perhaps why Jesus places forgiveness at the heart of the prayer he taught, which we know as the Lord's Prayer. 'Forgive us our sins,' the line goes – and that's important, but here's his vital counterpoint: 'for we ourselves forgive everyone indebted to us'.[1]

No Limits

Of course it doesn't take long for Jesus' Disciples to get around to the crunch question raised by his advocation of forgiveness: What are the limits of forgiveness? How many times do we forgive before we say, 'Enough!'? Seven times is Peter's not unreasonable suggestion. Famously, Jesus' answer is seventy times seven.[2] He's not saying that on the four hundred and ninety-first occasion of an offence, forgiveness is no longer required. Rather, the very big number is simply an indication that the requirement for forgiveness never stops! This is never, of course, to approve continued abuse or wrong-doing. Jesus is clear that we must address any wrong-doing (*From now on do not sin again*).[3] But it is a reminder that forgiveness remains the starting point for reconciliation.

If reconciliation is personal, it's also communal. This can be seen in the way that religious communities see themselves. Rather than being outside the wider community they will often see themselves as being at its (quiet, often unseen) heart, gently subverting

1 Luke 11.4.
2 Matthew 18.22.
3 John 8.11b.

the damaging aspects of the status quo, praying and acting for reconciliation, embodying and mediating the possibility of a new reconciled world starting here and now.

Reconciliation (Reconcile, be Reconciled): A Practice

So how can we practise the demanding business of *Reconciliation (Reconcile, be Reconciled)*? At the first stage in the spirit of the traditional practice this needs to begin in the small things. In the daily irritations and in the mundane conflicts – in the jostle for a parking space and in the debate over who does the washing up. This is where the practice of forgiveness begins to find its shape. This must be the starting point for all the wider reconciliations for which we are yearning. There are no short-cuts!

Going deeper into the tradition, the desire for a reconciled life finds dramatic shape in the sacrament of baptism. This act has been at the heart of the community that has aspired to follow Jesus since his own baptism by the wild desert prophet John (the Baptizer). By immersion (or in some traditions sprinkling) in water and the figurative washing away of all that requires forgiveness, the one being baptized is declaring his or her desire to follow in the way of Jesus the Christ, to be reconciled to God and to the communities of earth and saints. This is, of course, just the beginning of a journey that will last a life-time and beyond.[4] Forgiveness and reconciliation are demanding. But they are also sources of amazing freedom. And those who undergo baptism frequently experience a joyous sense of freedom.

If you sense a desire to consider this act of reconciliation, find a priest or minister of the Christian tradition to which you feel most connected or drawn and explore the possibility. If you are already baptized, perhaps in a christening service when you were

---

4 Pope Benedict XVI in *Porta Fidei* (Door of Faith), 2012: www.vatican.va/holy_father/benedict_xvi.

too young to remember it, a traditional way to keep on stepping back into this sign of reconciliation is to splash yourself with holy water from the font or from the stoup (usually a small bowl set into the wall) at the entrance to the church, as you make the sign of the cross. Each time we do this, another move towards reconciliation opens up. *Reconcile, be Reconciled!*

48

Sacramental Life
(Live the Brilliant Future Now)

WE MAY BE PIXIES

We may be pixies
but we might be giants!
not just lemonheads counting crows
but proclaimers
rolling stones smashing pumpkins
a clash, a joy division opening
doors onto nirvana

Very truly, I tell you, the one who believes in me will also do the works that I do and, in fact, will do greater works than these, because I am going to the Father.

A teaching of Jesus: John 14.12

Bold Shapes, Sweeping Lines

Bold shapes, sweeping lines, strong colours. I love the art of my sometime-collaborator Alison Berrett.[1] The wonder of whatever is all around us (often unseen or ignored) is being opened up. So that's what's happening beneath our feet! And all over the cosmos!

---

1 www.alisonberrett.co.uk.

Her work energizes me, and makes me feel that I can do pretty much anything, however tough, improbable or even impossible the future task might seem.

One of the core practices for those who set out on the Jesus path is the nurturing of a human life that in itself pictures and carries a story of hope. A life crafted like this becomes a kind of sacrament – at the same time both a sign of hope and a coming-into-being of the reality of the hope to which it points. It holds the tension that we all feel between the way things are and the possibility of what they may yet become. It shows how the former can open up into the latter. And it demonstrates how each and every human life can be part of the making-of-a-better-world-now.

Earlier in *Running over Rocks* we explored what it might be like to begin to re-imagine the world.[2] In this practice of *Sacramental Life (Live the Brilliant Future Now)* we are imagining how the making-of-a-better-world-now takes shape primarily in our lives as individuals, and then ripples out into the world. This is where words and actions meet, and it requires from us imagination and discipline, courage and humility. Live like this, says Jesus, and 'you will do greater works' than what has gone before. And this 'kingdom of heaven' is already happening. The brilliant but impossible future is already here! It's emerging everywhere. Around us, through us and, if need be, despite us; close by, and – vitally – among us, within us.[3] In the light of this revelation every act of transformation within us, however small, begins to take on greater significance. The brilliant future for the world can take shape in us now!

Into the Dreaming Space

For the earliest followers of Jesus the sacramental life was discovered through commitment to the path of the disciple. For other

---

2 See Practice 36, 'Re-imagine the World'.
3 Luke 17.21.

of Jesus' earliest followers it became called The Way. In the early centuries of the Church the development of this kind of life was a particularly costly path, and required a long period of serious preparation known as the catechumenate. The monastic life has always given (and created space for) a high degree of attention to the pursuit of the sacramental life. In the second half of the twentieth century renewed inspiration was taken in some streams of the tradition from the lives of the great Jewish prophets, seeing their dynamic re-imagining through words and action (often symbolic) as being a pattern for us to follow and emulate.

But perhaps the first step towards a sacramental life for many of us is to find the space to dream again. The impossibility of a truly good future may feel so solid and so absolute that all our dreaming has stopped. We each have to rediscover hope for ourselves – no-one can do it for us. The Christ path to enlightenment involves stepping again into the dreaming space, into the clearing in the forest that awaits us – and then welcoming others into the same space. Art has a particularly profound role to play in opening up the dreaming space. It can itself act as a sacrament of transformation, bringing about what it points towards. And through art the impossible but brilliant future is taking shape right now somewhere near you – on a bench in a studio, on an easel in a classroom, on a wall in a street, on a stage in a pub, in a chapel in a church – in spray paint and oil, in stone and bronze, in performance and in poetry, in sound and in silence. The re-imagining tradition continues to find new expression.

The Artist Jesus

Jesus was an artist. Not perhaps in the conventional sense, but as one in the long tradition of prophets who cast visions of an alternative world – absolutely! And his chief media are questions, stories and performance, each full of authenticity, space and imagination. In the way of any good artist, Jesus doesn't try to tell his listeners everything. Through his questions we are invited to work out what is true, to see what is happening, to imagine the impossible. What do you think? he asks. 'What do you want me to do for you?'[4] 'What are you looking for?'[5] 'Who are you looking for?'[6] 'Why are you afraid?'[7] And, intriguingly, 'Who do you say that I am?'[8]

His parables have a dynamic quality, always urging the listener to make the next move, leaving space for us to place ourselves within the story in our own setting. They invite us to do the imagining work with him. And two thousand years on, his symbolic actions – his performance artworks – continue to worry and inspire us, prod us and awaken us. There's the giving of thanks for a meal for thousands with almost nothing to offer them to eat.[9] The clearing of the temple: 'My house shall be called a house of prayer; but you are making it a den of robbers.'[10] And the stunning humility of a silent response before his accusers.[11] It's as if he's placing the pen, the brush and the chisel of re-imagining into our hands.

Sacramental Life (Live the Brilliant Future Now): A Practice

 At the first stage, seeking the spirit of *Sacramental Life (Live the Brilliant Future Now)*, this practice is about finding ways to explore and articulate how you experience the gaps between the way things are and the seemingly impossible future for which you might dream. Look for your own way – in words or in art perhaps– to explore this gap. Ask these questions of yourself and

---

4 Matthew 20.32.
5 John 1.38.
6 John 20.15.
7 Mark 4.40.
8 Mark 8.29.
9 Matthew 14.19.
10 Matthew 21.13.
11 Matthew 26.63.

others: How would you like the world around you to be different? And crucially, how could that change begin to take shape first in you?

Going deeper into the practice of the ancient tradition, begin to familiarize yourself with the old artists of the impossible future who inspired Jesus – the prophets of the Jewish scriptures and the Old Testament. Let them inspire you to ask questions, tell stories and act symbolically. What questions could you ask? What stories could you tell? What symbolic acts could you perform? How will your life take on new shape? Let them show you how to live the brilliant future now!

A further step still would be to explore the possibility of committing yourself to a course of catechumenate or discipleship. The monastics have accumulated extraordinary depths of experience and knowledge about how to nurture a sacramental life in the way of Jesus. Seek out a religious community and discover what may be possible where you are, or online. St Benedict, one of the great fathers of the Western monastic tradition, writes movingly in the Prologue to his Rule about the monastery as 'a school for the Lord's service':

Do not be daunted immediately by fear and run away from the road that leads to salvation at the outset. But as we progress in this way of life and in faith, we shall run on the path of God's commandments, our hearts overflowing with the inexpressible delight of love . . .[12]

---

12 *The Rule of St Benedict in English*, ed. T. Fry, Collegeville, MN: The Liturgical Press, 1982, p. 19.

49

Blessing (Become Blessing)

LET'S GO! A LITANY FOR THE NEW WORLD

let's go!
let's grow
let's go for a walk
let's not settle for talk
let's imagine new worlds
let's see fears unfurl
let's listen to dreams
let's paint the town green
let's spike guns with flowers
let's confront tyrants with prayers
let's meet abuse with blessing
let's hear people singing
let's nurture our wonder
let's pause to ponder
let's stand amazed
let's fall down dazed
let's love this place
let's be flooded with grace
let's meet hate with love
let's fly Picasso's dove
let's honour our labour
let's love God and neighbour
let's eat bread and drink wine
let's kiss and give time

let's grow
let's go!

Then Jesus led them out as far as Bethany, and, lifting up his hands, he blessed them.

From the life of Jesus: Luke 24.50

Just a Beginning

As I walk, something has caught my attention. Nothing spectacular today, just the beautiful and brilliant way in which the colours of the trees and fields seem to deepen as I approach them. Most days I take a walk from my home in south Devon, along the tidal road following the estuary, or over the hills behind the village. Whatever the weather, the time of the day, the season, I always feel remade. I return to my work energized and grateful. The landscape has blessed me. And, I hope, in some way I may now be better able to offer blessing to others as a result of this encounter with the earth.

The final act of Jesus, Luke tells us, was to bless his followers.[1] And this rag-tag group went on to change the world. The final act was thus just a beginning. And the blessing may not be incidental to that outcome. In the Jesus tradition there is an undeniable sense that in the act of blessing *something shifts* around us. A blessing is more than the words that are voiced, greater than any gesture made. Possibilities are being opened up in an ever-moving cosmos. So the practice of *Blessing (Become Blessing)* is about stepping into this tradition and into the world-changing possibility of blessing. It's about nurturing the act of blessing in our daily lives. And it's about letting the act of blessing change both the giver and the receiver so that we become blessing in our very being.

---

1 Luke 24.50–53.

Something Else is Going On

So what might be happening in the act of blessing? True blessing is never a power game. It's never a gift of the haves to the have-nots. A true blessing has a reciprocal quality. Blessing changes the one who blesses, and it changes the one who receives blessing. The act of blessing someone engages the spirit of compassion within the person offering blessing. And the receiving of blessing helps the person being blessed to step into the future that is waiting for them. True blessing gives dignity and worth to the person being blessed. It requires the giving of attention from the one giving blessing. This is equally true in a group setting as in a one-to-one context. Jesus' blessing of the Disciples carries weight because he knows the Disciples and cares for them. The blessing offered in the gathering of any Christ-community can equally be an experience like this. When the person offering the blessing looks into the faces of the people being blessed with compassion and care, even if she or he doesn't know them as individuals, the blessing can be one of integrity, bringing change.

Blessing signifies that something else is going on, beyond the limits of our concerns and fears, our actions and ideas. It suggests that there is a deeper reality of goodness at work. This might simply be the revelation that existence itself has a benevolent quality, that somehow everything will be OK. This is the kind of blessing I often experience as I walk in the valley and fields near my home. It is in itself good. But, even more intriguingly, in the Jesus tradition the practice of blessing signifies something about the nature of the divine, taking us into a long-lived experience that the community of God is close, that the community of God is personal, and that the community of God is good. And this goes beyond being just a *sign* of that belief in the true nature of things. The act of blessing is seen as also in some way *opening up* what it points to. Blessing has a sacramental quality. It is therefore serious and mysterious, a precious act that should be treated with care and reverence.

Balance, Grace and Momentum

In my experience the blessing can be one of the most profound moments in a gathering of people seeking to engage with the Jesus path. I've occasionally seen blessings dashed off, of course – the sooner to get out of here perhaps, or through a lack of sense of the stillpoint of the gathering – but whenever the blessing is given space, attention and reverence there can be a tangible sense of that *something shifting* as the words are said and gestures made. The possibility that a new world is being glimpsed is further emphasized by the wording of the blessing: it is usually a Trinitarian pattern, making clear that the blessing being invoked is that of the loving community of God, Father, Son and Holy Spirit. There's something very strong in the three-fold nature of these blessings. The repeated triplets have a natural balance, grace and momentum.

I really like the traditional accompaniment to blessing in this context, the making of the sign of the cross by both priest and people. In either case when I'm involved, I like to make the sign bigger rather than smaller, slower rather than faster, and deliberate rather than hurried. The physical act of blessing seems to emphasize the possibility of what is happening. You can feel the blessing becoming embodied. Like so many of the practices in *Running Over Rocks*, we need to *become* the thing that we are trying to practise. And in this way the formal blessing shared in the context of a religious ritual continues to ripple out into the wider world in other words, gestures and actions. The blessing gets passed on from person to person.

Blessing (Become Blessing): A Practice

 The first stage of the practice of *Blessing (Become Blessing)* is about nurturing something of the spirit of blessing wherever you are. Look for an opportunity each day to offer a simple action or phrase to someone that will be a blessing to them.

The next step takes us deeper into the ancient Jesus tradition. It also asks us to engage with our own context. Using a traditional Trinitarian blessing as a starting point, write or create a blessing in your own words and gestures, for the people in your own setting. Look for the right time to use it. And so may you *Become Blessing*!

PRACTICES OF LOVE

From fear towards love:
the beginning and the ending

What if it's all about love? What if life is one astonishing opportunity to learn to love and to be loved?

The final set of practices takes us back to the beginning and forward to the ending of everything. The Jesus path suggests that

life really is all about love: love for the earth and its creatures, for our fellow human beings, for life itself and for the divine. Intuitively, we know in our bones that love is always both the question and the answer. The song of love (and the love song) always endures, however much reality, disappointment or cynicism we throw at it.

We found this thick ship's rope washed up on the beach of St Columba's bay, Iona, and shaped it into a symbol of the Holy Trinity – the irresistible dance of God, source of all love.

What may be less instinctive but just as insightful is the possibility that love is the counter to all our fears. This set of practices helps us to rediscover love, and allow our experiences of love to shape the way that we live and the way that we bring good to the world.

The season connected with these Practices of Love is every season, every day, every moment. The Jesus tradition has discovered that Love is truly a practice for all seasons. That love has no limits. That love is irresistible . . .

50

Face Fear with Love

EVENING STAR (THE BELOVED DISCIPLE)

'the darkness has lifted' whispered
the frail evening star
as he held my hand and sought his breath
at the close of another long pondered day, truth
may come, a shone-through moment
when we may understand
that nothing else need be written in the sand
no other stories told, no other takes or mis-takes
except this most elemental of states:
to learn to love and to receive love
to carry love and to become love, so
'the darkness has lifted' whispered
the frail evening star
now full of light . . .

God is love, and those who abide in love abide in God, and God abides in them. There is no fear in love, but perfect love casts out fear.

A reflection on the life of Jesus: 1 John 4.16b, 18a

The Metal Box Dream

I'm drowning, in a metal box – a room in a sinking ship. The door has slammed shut, it has no internal handle, and there's no way out.

I wonder if a certain amount of fear is good for us? Perhaps we need a shot of fear every so often to feel fully alive. The popularity of horror movies indicates that possibility. I rarely have fearful dreams, so I take particular notice of them when they come – but even now I feel uncomfortable writing about this one. (Form an orderly queue to tell me what the dream suggests about me.)

Fear is, for most of us, a really strong driver. And it can easily come to dominate us. Earlier we explored the idea of fighting our dragons with humility.[1] We've also noted that occasionally the only thing that will enable us to hold on in tough times is to choose to be courageous and to do the right thing.[2] In this practice, one of the final three practices, each exploring the possibility of love, I want to suggest that the most freeing way to live with our fears is to face them with love – the only spirit that truly enables us to live as free people. For this reason we might say that the true opposite of fear is not calmness, confidence or even hope, but love.

The Disciple's Great Conclusion

It's some time near the end of the first century AD, and the aged disciple John is committing to words his decades-long reflections on the life and meaning of Jesus. The great conclusion of his Gospel and letters[3] seems to come to this: it's all about love. And, more specifically, God is love, and in the man Jesus God somehow has been with us, showing us what that love could be like, living out

---

1 See Practice 34, 'Fight Dragons, with Humility'.

2 See Practice 41, 'Choose Courageous'.

3 If we assume they are all by the same person – a reasonable assumption but not one shared by all scholars.

its possibilities and its implications. Those possibilities turned out to be full of freedom, the implications to be extremely demanding. True love brings deep goodness – but it may get you crucified. Love, for John, is the only way to a peaceable world. But it costs.

Love always has an outward momentum. At love's root is the desire to create the space for another to flourish. In any true love relationship the two lovers will always be looking for ways to encourage each other to become all that they can be, to step into their *Deep Flow*[4] and stay in their spirit.[5] Could it be that a stance of love within us might create necessary space for our fears to have their say? I'm really tempted to push away from memory my dream of drowning in a metal box. But if I face, even begin to *welcome*, that dream with love, perhaps there may be some giftedness enclosed within the fear. The bad dream may turn out to be a tough gift.

Stronger than Pretty Much Anything

If we are to face our fears with love – if love is to do its beautiful thing – we will need to let love begin to shape us. We need to *become* love, so that the boundary lines between love as something we do and love as something we are – love as our deep nature – become increasingly blurred. This is what the Jesus tradition thinks of as moving from *image* to *likeness*. In the tradition, humanity is created 'in the image of God'.[6] But the image is not all that we are made for. The image conveys the idea of the outward appearance. So being in the same image as the divine who is love means that we can *look something like love*. This is good and important. But the real thing, says the tradition and its teacher Jesus, is to *become love in our whole being*, internally as well as in outward appearance.

---

4 See Practice 24, 'Find Your Deep Flow'.
5 See Practice 30, 'Stay in Your Spirit'.
6 Genesis 1.27.

Let's talk about hats. I could wear an amber trilby today (I know where one can be purchased). It would, I think, say something about me. Even if it met with sartorial derision, I imagine that my amber trilby would convey a sense of joy. It might even help me to step into my joyfulness. But something deeper would need to be happening within me around the growth of joy for you to en-counter a truly joyful person in me. The hat is good, but it's just the image, just the beginning. We need to become love – and when that happens, everything becomes possible!

St Paul wrote movingly of the strength of love (and specifically of the love that is God and shown in Jesus) in a letter to the first community of followers of the Jesus Way in the imperial city of Rome. Like other early churches, this community was under great pressure and facing the threat of persecution when Paul wrote:

> For I am convinced that neither death, nor life, nor angels, nor rulers, nor things present, nor things to come, nor powers, nor height, nor depth, nor anything else in all creation, will be able to separate us from the love of God in Christ Jesus our Lord.[7]

Love, we might say, is stronger than pretty much anything.

Face Fear with Love: A Practice

 A first and necessary step in the practice of *Face Fear with Love* is to recognize our fears. We can then begin to respond to them with intention, rather than just with instinct. (Please note that there is still a place for the instinctive response of flight in certain situations – may you know when!) At the end of today ask yourself this (and your answer to this question may come as a shock but the insight may be worth the effort and

---

7 Romans 8.38–39.

indignity): To what extent have my actions and inactions today been shaped by fear? A next step is to convert the energy of fear (and fear carries a lot of energy) into something more positive. So, try to take the energy that comes from your fear of a certain situation happening and convert it into love for something or someone else. A further and even more radical approach is to reflect love back to the source of your fear. Experiment with this. Is it possible to return whatever is fearful that is coming your way with a measure of love? What might that look like? And so may you *Face Fear with Love.*

51

Embrace Intimacy

NORTHERN LIGHTS BETWEEN US SHINING

There are northern lights between us shining
tonight the skies are iridescent, lining
our dark horizons, igniting our hidden dawn.
Are we the only people looking up? Drawn
into a rippling curtain of light born
in some ancient solar storm,
the first light of our coming-into-being
now the flicker of some new imagining
carrying us into shimmering day
seeing our darkness fade away.
So North Utsire and South Utsire
Fair Isle and Viking
Hebrides and Malin
become one, and they are us.
There are northern lights between us shining.

Then Jesus poured water into a basin and began to wash the dis-
ciples' feet and to wipe them with the towel that was tied around
him.

From the life of Jesus: John 13.5

A Primal Dream

I love you. One simple phrase that is being uttered many times all over the planet as you read this. *I love you* awakens old dreams, and brings new worlds into being. So much of our possibility as human beings is connected to our desire for intimacy – for the love of another, for connection and belonging, for unity and at-oneness, without defence or fear, without shame or anxiety. Intimacy is vital for our well-being. But intimacy can be demanding. The gifts of intimacy can also be its uncomfortable challenges. Are we up for vulnerability, for letting go of control, for letting the other be the other? The practice of *Embrace Intimacy* is about (re)discovering the vitality of intimacy for ourselves – intimacy with another human being, intimacy with the earth, and intimacy with God – and allowing that intimacy to enable us to bring good to the world.

In the Jesus tradition our impulse towards intimacy is seen as the awakening of a primal dream, a profound movement into our deeper belonging, to each other, to the earth and to the mystery that we call God. It suggests that our desire for intimacy is both a sign of our desire for oneness and a means by which we can step into the reality of that oneness. In the Jewish scriptures, the core-texts used by Jesus in the formation of his teaching, there's an astonishing and beautiful exploration into a life of intimacy in the Song of Songs. It's clearly about love and sex. It's also about intimate relationships between humanity, the earth[1] and the divine.

Becoming at One With

In the practice *Cave of the Heart (Nurture your Contemplative)*[2] I suggested that the contemplative experience may be about letting the divine *happen to us*, our *being with* the divine, and a

---

1 I believe that the earth context and earth metaphors in Song of Songs – mountains, garden, trees and fruit – are not incidental for this exploration of intimacy.

2 See Practice 46, 'Cave of the Heart (Nurture Your Contemplative)'.

re-orientation of our being. There may be an even deeper experience waiting for us. This is the possibility of *becoming one with* the divine. The late fourth-century teacher intriguingly known as Pseudo-Macarius says that, in prayer, 'the soul is linked with the Lord, and the Lord, full of compassion and love, unites himself to it. Then the soul and the Lord are one spiritually, they form one life, one heart.'[3] So in contemplation there is an intimate coming together as one between divinity and humanity. Old dreams awaken, new worlds come into being!

Our experience of sex is probably our most earthy passionate expression of oneness. In all its wonder, beauty and bliss – and yes, even within or despite its awkwardness, disappointment or humour – sex can be a sublime experience of at-oneness. In both its seasons of welcome presence and yearning absence, our sex and our desire for sex open up the nature of our belonging. This search for oneness reveals a deep connection between sex and contemplation. Both reflect and both meet our yearning for intimacy. Both require us to be truly ourselves. Both require us to be vulnerable, to give ourselves away. Both require us to allow the other to be whoever they are. Both need us to receive the other. Both offer the possibility of a becoming-at-one-with the other. And because both require a true honouring of the mystery of the other, they need to be approached with tenderness.

Love Me Tender

Tenderness can be hard to find. Worn down by the toughness of events, we can so easily lose our tenderness. But a necessary step in moving from fear towards love is a commitment to live with tenderness – in all areas of life. In his pursuit of the Jesus path the sixteenth-century Spanish friar St John of the Cross is one of the great explorers into the life of tenderness. In his writings he reveals

---

3 Quoted in Olivier Clement, *The Roots of Christian Mysticism*, London: New City, 1993.

the passionate nature of the spiritual life. His poems – 'Songs of the soul in intimate union with God' is one description used of them – are extravagant, moving, undeniably erotic, but always tender. 'So tenderly your love becomes my own,' he writes in 'The Living Flame'. I find this deeply moving and persuasive. So I want to encourage a renewed openness to understanding our relationship with the divine as being a journey of intimacy, and to experiencing the religious life as a passionate thing. Actually this is how it has always been experienced by a minority, even if this truth has been suppressed or ignored as being too messy, too difficult, or too embarrassing.

The Jesus stance of tenderness is something to be nurtured as a way of being, but must take shape in authentic words and actions. There's a poignant story from the life of Jesus which exemplifies tenderness-in-action.[4] It's the last night of his freedom, shortly before what we know as the Last Supper. In an act of simple, tender humility and care, Jesus himself takes on a traditional servant role, and washes the feet of the Disciples. Not only is Jesus subverting the expected relationship of teacher–student and master–servant, he is finding a way for his love for his followers and companions to take on a simple but tender shape. Pouring water into a basin, a towel wrapped around his waist, the Master washes the feet of the Disciples. And so, he says, 'you also should do as I have done to you'.[5]

Embrace Intimacy: A Practice

Begin this practice by reflecting on your own recent experiences of intimacy. To what extent have these been characterized by attention, vulnerability, honesty and tenderness? If you are without a partner your yearning for intimacy must not be

---

4 John 13.1–20.
5 John 13.15b.

ignored.[6] And if you do have a partner true intimacy needs to be a reciprocal thing, nurtured within a wider environment of commitment and devotion.[7] There is currently a great openness, both for better and for worse, around sex and sexuality. Within that culture of openness we need, for a better world, to see a renewed emphasis on the nurturing of true intimacy and tenderness. It starts, of course, with each one of us. So *Embrace Intimacy*!

---

6 If we are on our own, both for our own well-being and for the goodness we may bring to the world, it seems to me important that we do not retreat into an intimacy-free zone. With regard to sex, if we are not called to a celibate life, this may involve discerning how our sexuality could be expressed on our own, with love and tenderness.

7 See Ian Adams, *Cave Refectory Road: Monastic rhythms for contemporary living*, London: Canterbury Press, 2010, pp. 68–74 for more on a life of devotion.

52

Give Everything to Find Everything

THE DIG: SOMETHING STILL SHINES

In bleached bone middens
in scraped shell heaps, hidden
in dried dirt decaying
under layers of burning
through lost ages of occupation
of building and destruction –
unimagined or forgotten
something still shines.

So scrape off the soil,
put in a trench
bring up to the light,
lay out on a bench
each smashed pot
each toothless comb
each twisted nail
each fragment of bone
and dig to discover
unimagined or forgotten
the something that still shines –
and always will.

The kingdom of heaven is like treasure hidden in a field, which someone found and hid; then in his joy he goes and sells all that he has and buys that field.

A parable of Jesus: Matthew 13.44

What You Already Sensed?

I hope this book may have confirmed many things that you have already sensed deep within you – your own deep belonging in a wonderful world, the immense capacity of this earth and its creatures for goodness, and the triumph of love over its many opposites. I hope you have found inspiration and resources for playing your part in the Great Task of Our Time: *to be goodness and to bring goodness* – to become fully human. I hope it may have reinforced your sense that you are already part of this momentum for good! And that there is much awaiting you – to receive goodness, to carry it, to share it. And I hope that you have been moved and inspired by the wisdom, practice and even the presence of Jesus, who is always saying to us with great love, humility and compassion, 'You are the light of the world',[1] 'Follow me',[2] 'I am with you always'.[3]

One of the greatest (and shortest) of short stories ever told is Jesus' parable of treasure in the field. The treasure is worth everything. It seems to me that our potential involvement in the bringing of good to the world is truly worth all that we have. That we really need to be ready to *Give Everything to Find Everything*. And the word *give* is vital here. Many of the practices here, rooted in the life and wisdom of Jesus, involve a giving away, a letting go, an opening of hands and heart, a dropping away of what we instinctively want to hold close, usually because of fear. Please remember that

---

1 Matthew 5.14.

2 Matthew 9.9.

3 Matthew 28.20.

this giving-away movement is not a one-off transaction. The call to give everything is daily. This is demanding. But it's also about movement not achievement. So it's very possible. Every day is another opportunity to re-orient ourselves with humility and love in the direction of our brothers and sisters, our fellow creatures and the planet, and the divine. To take our place of connectedness.

Give Everything to Find Everything: A Practice

 In many areas of life moderation and balance are really important. I'm going to suggest that this is not one of those. Rather, that our desire to *be goodness* and to *bring goodness*, to live with imagination, adventure and generosity, to *become truly human* – requires all our attention. It only calls for everything!

The practice of *Give Everything to Find Everything* is about establishing a ritual by which you remind yourself each day of your desire to give everything to find everything, to become the truly human being you are meant to be and to bring good to the world. Only you can decide what your ritual will look like. But I would encourage you to make it physical in some way, perhaps through a gesture or movement, accompanied by words. Make it simple and portable so that you can do it wherever you are.

My own daily practice of *Give Everything to Find Everything* is to move through a simple series of postures while centring myself in the Beatitudes[4] – the sayings of Jesus at the heart of his wisdom and practice. May they become a centring point for you too, as you seek to bring goodness to the world:

Blessed are the poor in spirit, for theirs is the kingdom of heaven.
Blessed are those who mourn, for they will be comforted.
Blessed are the meek, for they will inherit the earth.

4 See www.belovedlife.org for more information.

Blessed are those who hunger and thirst for righteousness, for
    they will be filled.
Blessed are the merciful, for they will receive mercy.
Blessed are the pure in heart, for they will see God.
Blessed are the peacemakers, for they will be called children of
    God.
Blessed are those who are persecuted for righteousness sake,
    for theirs is the kingdom of heaven.
You are the salt of the earth.
You are the light of the world.[5]

Something Still Shines

Sometimes our shining self can seem stubbornly remote. Buried
deep under all our stuff, or forgotten under whatever we have come
to believe about ourselves. The smashed pot, the toothless comb,
the twisted nail and the fragment of bone seem to be dominant.
But the something that still shines is there all the time, waiting to
be brought to the light, lovingly restored and offered once more as
a gift to the world . . .

    May you give everything and may you find everything.
    May you be goodness and may you bring goodness.
    May you run over rocks, light and free
    laughing at the brilliance of it all . . .

---

5 Matthew 5.3–10, 13a, 14a.